Trevethl

A Cornish S

Volume 3

William Davy Watson

Alpha Editions

This edition published in 2024

ISBN : 9789362090362

Design and Setting By
Alpha Editions
www.alphaedis.com
Email - info@alphaedis.com

As per information held with us this book is in Public Domain.
This book is a reproduction of an important historical work. Alpha Editions uses the
best technology to reproduce historical work in the same manner it was first
published to preserve its original nature. Any marks or number seen are left
intentionally to preserve its true form.

Contents

VOLUME 3 ....- 1 -

CHAPTER I. ....- 3 -

CHAPTER II. ....- 7 -

CHAPTER III. ....- 13 -

CHAPTER IV. ....- 18 -

CHAPTER V. ....- 23 -

CHAPTER VI. ....- 29 -

CHAPTER VII. ....- 35 -

CHAPTER VIII. ....- 42 -

CHAPTER IX. ....- 47 -

CHAPTER X. ....- 51 -

CHAPTER XI. ....- 57 -

CHAPTER XII. ....- 63 -

CHAPTER XIII. ....- 70 -

CHAPTER XIV. ....- 78 -

CHAPTER XV ....- 84 -

CHAPTER XVI. ....- 90 -

CHAPTER XVII. ....- 96 -

VOLUME 3

CHAPTER I.

Menenius. What work's, my countrymen, in hand? Where go you with bats and clubs? The matter? Speak, I pray you.

Citizen. Our business is not unknown to the senate; they have had inkling, this fortnight, what we intend to do, which now we'll show 'em in deeds. They say poor suitors have strong breath: they shall know we have strong arms too.

SHAKSPEARE.

Among the most striking features of the scenery of West Cornwall, are the fantastic piles of bare granite which rise occasionally from the summit of an upland, and to a distant spectator present the exact semblance of a castle, with towers, turrets, and outworks. So a stranger, standing on Cape Cornwall and looking towards the Land's End, might imagine he there beheld the fortress whose sanguinary sieges obtained for that promontory its ancient name of the Headland of Blood. Or again, reclining on the moorland, near the cromlech of Morvah, while the sun was sinking behind Carnyorth, he might fancy that at the red-edged battlements on the ridge, the original inhabitants of the country made their last stand against the invaders from the German Ocean.

Approach soon destroys the illusion. And it is superfluous to observe that the warriors of those times had no notion of the structures which these caprices of nature mimic—the castles of our Plantagenets and Tudors. Their real fortresses still exist to afford employment to the antiquary, and inspiration to the poet; and to one of them we now invite the reader to accompany us.

Castle Dinas occupies the crest of the highest ground between the picturesque village of Gulvall and the pilchard-perfumed town of St. Ives, and commands an uninterrupted view both of Mount's Bay and of the Irish Sea. Two concentric ramparts of unhewn stones, flung together more rudely than a Parisian barricade, exhibiting the science of fortification in its very infancy, inclose a circular area of considerable extent. From it the ground slopes, not very rapidly, on all sides; and as there are no screens, an occupant of the camp can see an approaching friend or enemy some time before he arrives. Within the inner circle some prosaic favourer of picnics has erected a square *folly*, with a turret at each angle, not harmonizing very well with local associations, but convenient in case of a shower of rain.

Around the folly, on the night which followed the departure of the orphans of Trevethlan from the home of their fathers, was pacing a stalwart man of weather-beaten aspect, with an impatient and irregular gait. The sun had sunk below the horizon, and all the south and west quarters of the sky were covered with heavy masses of cloud, from behind which, at intervals, came the low mutterings of distant thunder. Flashes of lightning followed one another in quick succession, becoming more and more brilliant as the shades of evening grew deeper. They broke from various quarters of the horizon, but particularly from the point of sunset. The light seemed to flit or be reflected all round the sky. Sometimes it was a lambent flame of blue, sometimes a flush of faint rose colour; sometimes the dark clouds were displayed in bold relief against a bright sheet of yellow or white. So far the sea was still calm, and the air close and heavy. But at length there came a motion in the hot atmosphere. The surface of the water was crisped. A sigh wailed along it, as if the spirit of the tempest mourned over his mission; and then the storm, whose advent had been foreseen by Randolph and Helen, during their last visit to Merlin's Cave, advanced rapidly up the sky.

And a tempest scarcely less fierce raged in the breast of Gabriel Denis, as he paced hurriedly within those old ramparts. He was expecting an assembly almost as tumultuous as that of the warriors whose battle shouts once resounded there, and he was resolved that it should not disperse in the same innocuous manner as former meetings of the same character. One by one, and two by two, as the darkness deepened, his promised adherents arrived, and the ancient camp became filled with an excited mob, anxious for mischief, ignorant what to do.

Well might Randolph caution Edward Owen that in joining such musters as these he might easily be carried much further than he intended to go. A fretting population always contains inflammable materials, and it is far less difficult to kindle than to extinguish its fury. The consciousness of this fact frequently deters mob-leaders from urging their followers into a course where there will be no subsequent control.

And crimes of this nature are among the greatest that can be committed, especially in a free state. An idea prevails that there is a sort of heroism in defying public authority, no matter how trivial the occasion, nor how impotent the assailant. Defeated and punished, the criminal is not seldom regarded as a martyr. He is considered the victim of his own conscientiousness. Antecedent cases of successful sedition are quoted to justify subsequent failures. But all this is false and mischievous. There is never heroism in fool-hardiness: the so-styled martyr may witness to no truth: the conscientiousness may be of the kind which calls property a theft. And former successes are rather warnings than examples. Precedent cannot avail against the powers that be.

The assembly at Castle Dinas, however, was rather riotous than seditious, and uncertain in what direction to vent its desire for mischief. There was plenty of tinder, but no one to throw the spark; until Gabriel Denis, burning with the desire of revenge for the spoiling of his house and the death of his wife, joined the counsels of the malcontents, and brought into them the energy they had previously wanted. He now flung a firebrand among the rabble, and dozens of hands were stretched to seize it. It was just suited to the mood of the moment.

"To Lelant!" the smuggler shouted. "Why loiter we here on the hill, doing nothing either of good for ourselves or of ill for those who would put us down? Are we not many, and they few? To Lelant, I say. Let us turn the tables on the revenue thieves. They have plenty of mine in their stores; but I want not that. Drink it, lads, free of duty and free of charge. But there is a desolate home yonder on the bank. What stain is that on the floor?—there shall be a redder in the storehouse at Lelant. Ay, lads, let us to Lelant."

There was a great stir in the crowd: not a few voices echoed the smuggler's watchword—To Lelant: some of the men pressed forward as if eager to start: Gabriel himself turned to lead the way. But another voice arose: it came from the midst of a small and compact party on the outskirts of the meeting.

"What are ye about?" the speaker said. "Why go among the cutlasses and carbines? Is it the drink ye would have—the drink and the sport? Ye can get them cheaper than at Lelant. Look to our great houses. Does Gabriel say they have spoiled his? Let us spoil one of theirs. What say ye to Pendar'l?"

A shout, much more enthusiastic than that which hailed the smuggler's proposition, greeted this burst of eloquence.

"See!" continued the orator, "there's a storm coming up from the sea. It will hide our advance; and the soldiers are called away to the 'sizes. Let us disperse, and meet again on the grass of Pendar'l."

So said, so done. As the crowd moved off, it might be noted that there were some audible murmurs of "Trevethlan for ever!" "Hurrah for Trevethlan!" showing that at least a portion of the assembly were thinking of what had happened in that hamlet a few hours before. And then the multitude divided itself spontaneously into various parties, some proceeding by the lanes and other byways, and some boldly crossing the country in twos and threes;—silent, but not so regular, as an army of ants. Meantime the storm, driven along by a high wind, came up the sky, and before the foremost of the marauders had reached the park wall of Pendarrel, the rain was falling in torrents, and the thunder rolling overhead. But these were trifles to the hardy assailants, who were now fairly on fire, and had a definite object before their eyes. They scaled the wall wherever they first found it, and advanced through the grounds towards the hall, scaring the deer with the unwonted invasion. At length they found themselves re-united for the most part in a semicircle, investing all one side of the house. Fair and stately it stood amidst the trim pleasure-grounds, reflecting the vivid flashes of lightning from its white walls and many windows, and offering, alas! too tempting a prize to the lawless band around it. Within, the household were collected about their fire-sides, listening to the uproar of the storm, and little deeming that a more terrible enemy was at hand.

CHAPTER II.

When tumult lately burst his prison door,
And set plebeian thousands in a roar,
When he usurped authority's just place,
And dared to look his master in the face,
Liberty blushed, and hung her drooping head,
Beheld his progress with the deepest dread,
Blushed that effects like these she should produce,
Worse than the deeds of galley-slaves let loose:
She loses in such scenes her very name,
And fierce licentiousness must bear the blame.

COWPER.

"What can make the dogs bark in this manner?" exclaimed Mrs. Pendarrel to her husband and daughter. "Surely not the thunder."

"I cannot tell what it is, my dear," answered her spouse, who was nearly asleep after his return from Bodmin, in spite of the external uproar. "I wish they and the thunder would both be quiet."

Mildred went behind the curtains of a window. Thick as they were, the flashes of lightning had yet gleamed through them.

"What a tremendous night!" she exclaimed.

"Come from the window, Mildred," said Mrs. Pendarrel; "it is dangerous to stand there."

"Ha!" cried the daughter, "there is fire. It cannot be the lightning! Mamma! Papa!"

The urgency of her tone brought them both to the window. A red glare streamed over the lawn, and shone bright upon the dripping trees. Fire was there indeed.

Gabriel Denis, by this time wild with passion and excitement, had soon discovered the means of gratifying his turbulent desires. A range of farming offices, with some ricks, stretched to the west, and therefore to windward, of the hall. Let these be once kindled, and inactivity would soon give way to riot and confusion. The smuggler had not forgotten his tinder-box. He crept down into the homestead, found a convenient nook, and soon lighted a flame, which nothing but the speediest and most energetic exertion could hinder the furious wind from converting into a great conflagration.

Unhappily the tempest, closing doors and fastening shutters, prevented an immediate discovery of the blaze, and the heavy rain was powerless to check its progress under the fanning of the gale. The interior of the corn-stack, fired by Gabriel, rapidly became a furnace, while volumes of steam and smoke rolled from the wetted thatch, and were shortly followed by jets of flame bursting from the inside. Then masses of burning straw were lifted aloft by the wind and cast on the neighbouring ricks and wooden barns, and in scarcely more time than is occupied by this description, the homestead was evidently doomed to destruction, and the safety of the hall was become very problematical.

It was just then that Mildred summoned her father and mother to the window.

"Hark!" she said, "Was not that a shout? See, there are people running across the lawn, and under the trees. But, oh, what a light!"

Terrified domestics rushed into the parlour.

"The house is beset—hundreds of men—What can be done? What can be done?"

These exclamations were mingled with loud cries of "fire," from within and without the mansion. In the confusion, Esther Pendarrel seemed alone to preserve her presence of mind.

"Done!" she said. "The engine! The horses! Ride! Run! To Helston, and to Marazione! Raise the people! Bring down the soldiers! Away with you; and let us see where the fire is. And you, sir, look to your arms. Beset! Nonsense!"

So saying, Esther proceeded to the wing of the hall next to the farm offices, which could not be seen from the living rooms, while her husband hurriedly distributed his fire-arms among the few servants who remained, when their fellows had departed to endeavour to fulfil the injunctions of their mistress.

Mildred accompanied her mother. "Fie," said the latter, seizing by the wrist one of a group of maids who were crying in terror, "fie, girl! Be silent; let us have no confusion. We want all our nerve."

One glance from the window to which she went showed Esther the full extent of the calamity. Long tongues of fire, bending and quivering in the fierce wind, were licking the roof of a low range of outhouses which connected the farm-yard with the hall. Esther remembered that there was a door of communication between these buildings and the house itself. Unless they could be pulled down, and that instantly, the mansion would be in imminent peril. And besides, behind them were the ricks and barns, vomiting a perfect sea of fire, from which large flakes were ever and anon borne by the gale over the hall. One such struck the window where Mrs. Pendarrel stood with her daughter, and made them start back for a moment. And what hope was there of help? By the red glare they could see men clustered about, either gazing on the flames with indifference, or exhibiting exultation in their gestures and movements. Amidst the crackling of the fire and the thunder of the storm, they could hear the savage hurrahs of the incendiaries. Whence, then, could come help?

"We are lost, my child!" Esther said quietly. "But I presume they do not intend to burn us as well as the hall. Courage, dear."

She threw her arm round Mildred's waist, and led her back to the main stairs. There they found Mr. Pendarrel, and two or three men-servants, armed, but undetermined what to do.

"Husband," Esther whispered, "in five minutes all the west wing will be in flames. Nothing can save us, unless the troops arrive in time. Where are the girls? They must all be here."

The last words were spoken aloud.

"I will call them, mother," Mildred said; and she ran back to the offices.

"We have no chance," Esther continued as before, "unless the ruffians should turn——Hush! Hark!"

There was a clatter of steps to the door of the hall, succeeded by a loud knocking.

"Be ready," said Esther. "Let us not be outraged."

"Shall we not escape?" her husband asked. "By the back windows——"

"Are the maids all here? Where's Mildred?"

"I am here, dear mother," was the breathless reply, "and so are they."

"Then let us go," said Esther sadly. "Go through the drawing-rooms. To meet at the chief lodge. And you, my friends, will guard us as best you may. But for the fire, we might do more. All now would be in vain."

Bare-headed, the little party went out into the storm. Esther stoutly maintained her own heart, but she had much ado to keep up the courage of her companions. With quick but faltering steps they made their way through the shrubbery, in the direction Mrs. Pendarrel had indicated; looking back with hasty glances, and perceiving that the flames were now flying over the roof of the mansion, the west wing having already become their spoil. A little more delay, and perhaps escape had been impossible. And there were other dangers besides the fire.

The fugitives had just turned round the corner of a thick clump of laurels, when they found themselves in the presence of a crowd of men, who immediately surrounded them, preventing their further progress, insulting them both with words and gestures. Mr. Pendarrel, bewildered, fired a pistol, and the rabble rushed in upon him and those with him, incensed and excited beyond all control. It was a moment of despair. Esther pressed her daughter to her breast, and opposed herself to the assailants. Her husband, also, and the men-servants maintained a manful struggle. But numbers were prevailing, when the ruffians were themselves attacked in the rear. A throng of country people, apparently acting in concert, charged them suddenly, and with the first attack, drove them clear of their intended victims.

"Fly, madam," then said a voice beside Mrs. Pendarrel. "Fly. There are none now but friends in the way. And remember Edward Owen."

And Esther acted instantly on the advice, knowing that, whether true or false, it afforded the only hope for safety.

In the mean time, the hall-door had yielded to its assailants, and ruffianism triumphed through the mansion. Some fellows made their way to the cellars, and drank desperately, while others rioted through the various apartments in search of more valuable booty. Not a few quarrels arose for the possession of some portable trinket, upon which two of the marauders might have seized at once. Shouts and screams, and execrations resounded on all sides. And above them all rose the crackle of the advancing flames, not unlikely to inflict a well-merited doom upon some of those who exulted in them.

But many of the country-folks, aroused by the emissaries who escaped from the hall at the first alarm, had thronged to render assistance in subduing the flames. They were, however, disconcerted at finding themselves intercepted by a mob, whose intentions were precisely the reverse of their own. Coming singly or in small knots, without any community of action, they were unable to make any impression upon the banded ruffians, and they either departed to seek further aid, or became passive spectators of the ruin that was befalling Pendarrel.

There was one, however, of a different mood. Edward Owen, although he had attended the meeting at Castle Dinas, and accompanied the mob, shuddered at the devastation before him. So soon did he experience the truth of Randolph's words. Recoiling too late, but desirous to atone if possible for what was past, he hovered on the skirts of the crowd, and soon collected a tolerably formidable body of the well-disposed, with which to repress further outrage. They made their first show of prowess in rescuing the fugitive family: but beyond this their efforts were unavailing: the fire had obtained too great a head to be withstood.

The main fury of the storm had now passed; the rain had nearly ceased, and the wind had fallen; the lightning still flashed, and the thunder muttered in the east, while the western sky was once more becoming clear. But the flashes were too faint to be seen, and the muttering too low to be heard, in the bright glare and loud crackling of the flames that were devouring Pendarrel Hall. All the centre of the mansion, containing the great stairs and principal apartments, was in full conflagration. From window after window, as the glass flew under the heat, a long stream of fire shot forth, joining the ruddy blaze that broke from the roof. Once, a human form appeared in the midst of such a torrent, flinging its arms about in wild supplication for a few moments, and disappearing, either within or without. Above the house curled vast volumes of smoke, black, white, and yellow, filled with sparkling fragments, and glowing in the light of the flames. A flock of pigeons fled to and fro over the bright vapour, and every now and then a bird dashed into it, and dropped as if shot. Round about, on all sides, as near as the heat permitted, rushed the incendiaries, exulting in the destruction they had accomplished, and hailing every fresh burst of fire with frantic acclamations. Behind, at a little distance, the trees, still streaming with the recent rain, reflected the red glare from every branch. Farther off, a cottage window or a white wall, lighted more dimly, might denote the rising ground of the neighbourhood. And over all, were the dark clouds of the retreating tempest, the fury of which had that night caused no catastrophe so disastrous as was here wrought by the hand of man.

The family, so rudely driven from their home, succeeded in reaching the lodge designated by Esther for their rendezvous. Faint with excitement— even Mrs. Pendarrel's spirit failed her when she was safe from immediate peril—exhausted by their flight, deluged with the rain, they met together in a small room of the cottage, round a window which looked towards their late abode. With a sort of vacant despair they watched the flames which rose above the intervening trees, and showed the progress of ruin. The hall itself they could not see. Mildred sat, leaning upon her mother's shoulder, and holding her hand, while Mr. Pendarrel rested against the side of the casement. Not a word was spoken; and the only sounds that broke the silence of the lodge, were the subdued noise of the flames, and the shouts of the marauders.

But Mr. Pendarrel, with his ear against the wall, has now caught another sound; regular, rhythmical, advancing along the road. Nearer it came, and nearer, and before the listener had changed his position, a squadron of dragoons passed the lodge on a hand-gallop, and were followed by fire-engines. Alas! why came they no sooner?

The messengers who had made their way from the hall at the first discovery of the fire, sped fast away to Helston, looking back at intervals towards the light in the sky. The distance was about five miles; the road was slippery with the wet; the flood of rain was almost blinding: a full hour had elapsed before the first of the runners shouted "fire" in the deserted streets of the little borough. The inhabitants were at rest, but few were asleep, the din of the storm preventing slumber. Night-capped heads peeped timidly from windows, and demanded—where? The messenger learned the officers' quarters. There was some little demur. False alarms had been given before. But the bugle soon sounded to horse. The drowsy firemen equipped their engines; and when once the cavalcade had started, rattling over the stony street, a very short space sufficed to bring it to the gates of Pendarrel.

The greater portion of the marauders, struck with consternation at the sight of the soldiery, fled among the trees of the park, to be denounced, perhaps, at a future day, by informing comrades. But a few, maddened by intoxication and excitement, offered a futile resistance, and were captured on the spot, to answer for their ruffianism, not improbably with their lives.

As for the engines, they could effect nothing. The well-disposed of the country people, who were by this time assembled in great numbers, assisted in bringing them into play, and water was obtained from an ornamental reservoir in the garden; but fire was master of the hall. To save a small quantity of furniture from the lower rooms in the eastern wing, and to collect articles which lay scattered on the lawns, was all that the utmost exertion could accomplish. The whole of the mansion had fallen in, and the burning would continue as long as there remained anything to furnish fuel. Blackened walls, open to the sky, containing nothing but smoking and smouldering ruin, would be all the morning sun would shine upon of Pendarrel Hall.

CHAPTER III.

The Hall of Cynddylan is gloomy this night,
Without fire, without bed—
I must weep awhile, and then be silent.

The Hall of Cynddylan is gloomy this night,
Without fire, without candle—
Except God doth, who will endue me with patience?

LLYWARCH HEN, *by Owen.*

The destruction of Pendarrel Hall was the crowning outrage of the riotous. It was a crime for which a severe retribution was certain to be exacted. On information, given partly by the prisoners taken at the fire, partly by volunteers who hoped to screen themselves, the civil and military authorities swept the country far and wide, and arrested numbers of suspected individuals. The hamlet of Trevethlan felt the visitation, and among its accused was the unfortunate Edward Owen. Many people, shuddering at the consciousness of guilt, fled for shelter to the wild moors and desolate carns, or lurked in the caverns of the sea-shore, obtaining a scanty and precarious nourishment from venturous friends or kindred. The prime mover of all the mischief, Gabriel Denis, had been captured on the spot; and there was scarcely a cottage between the two seas, which did not miss from the family circle some son or brother now lying in prison or lurking in the waste.

On the night of the disaster, the Pendarrels were at last persuaded to seek repose in such accommodation as was afforded by the lodge; but sleep was out of the question. Jaded and sad, they met in the morning, and went forth to survey the ruins of their home. Melancholy enough was the mere destruction of the edifice, yet that was the least among their sorrows. Wealth might restore the house to all its former splendour, but other losses were irreparable. All the relics of bygone days; the pledges of friendship and of love, the trinkets associated with old personal reminiscences, the memorials of travel and adventure, the rarities collected with their own hands, the family heir-looms, the toys of one childhood laid by to amuse another, the books of early lessons and early leisure, the sketches and drawings, the portraits and miniatures of the dead,—all of these had perished, and could never be replaced; for Pendarrel was their home, their old familiar dwelling-place, the storehouse of all things dear,—their cradle and their grave. Other houses they had, but none like Pendarrel.

Even the stern pride of Esther might bend a little under so great a calamity. Only the morning before she had been exulting over the humiliation of Trevethlan, and now her own hearth was desolate. In the terror of the night she had been surprised into an unusual display of tenderness towards her daughter. But any such feelings were merely transitory. Tale-bearers soon brought to her ear the shouts of "Hurrah for Trevethlan," which had been heard among the rioters. She thought of the scornful silence with which her invitation of yesterday had been received at the Castle, and permitted herself to suspect that the night's outrage might have had more than empty sympathy from its inmates.

She perceived also, with impatience, that the event would necessarily postpone the marriage of her daughter, and require it to be celebrated in London. Both the delay and the place was obnoxious, because the watchful mother still feared that Mildred's outward docility covered a strong resolve, and she was sorry to restore her to the protecting influence of Mrs. Winston. Such were the cold and harsh thoughts, which in Mrs. Pendarrel succeeded to the first depression occasioned by the calamity. But coming so suddenly on her triumph, it would be strange indeed if it were wholly unfelt, and the sequel may show that its effects were more considerable than Esther suspected at the time.

The exiles selected one from a host of offers of hospitality, but only availed themselves of the shelter for a single night; setting out the following morning on their way to town, and arriving in May Fair in due course. Mrs. Winston awaited their coming. She had her full share of the recent catastrophe. True it was she had made another home for herself, but much of her heart remained at Pendarrel. Even in a lately-written letter Mildred had mentioned their partnership in books. In fact, the fire might long be remembered in the annals of the family, becoming an epoch to date from, like that commemorated among the Jews by the spot left bare in the decoration of their walls, "the memory of desolation."

In the first *tête-à-tête* between the sisters, they turned from their own misfortunes to that which had befallen their cousins of Trevethlan, and when Gertrude had mentioned the invitation which she had already despatched to Helen, Mildred suffered herself to be drawn into a confession of all that had passed under the hawthorns on the cliff.

"Ah, Mildred," her sister said, shaking her head in gentle reproof, "remember that while I will do anything to save you from a union you dislike, I will do nothing to promote one which our parents disapprove. And that I fear will be the case as regards this gentleman. Count nothing, my dear, from my invitation to his sister. I should, perhaps, have hesitated to give it, had I known the state of the case."

But Mildred heard this little lecture without much heeding its warning. She was meditating on designs of her own, which she had no intention of confiding even to her sister. Her mother was not at all unlikely to find that she had raised a devil which she would be unable to lay.

Mildred rejoiced, however, at one circumstance: her unwelcome suitor did not immediately follow her to London. He had not been present at the fire; for although his domains joined those of Pendarrel, the houses were very far apart; and there was sufficient uncertainty at Tolpeden respecting the locality of the flames to excuse the indolent coxcomb from proceeding to assist, an excuse of which he readily availed himself in the midst of such a storm. He was greatly vexed when he heard the truth in the morning, and he paid a visit of polite condolence to the family, at which, however, he was not favoured with the company of Mildred.

And he was far from impatient to accompany her to town. The gossips at Mrs. Pendarrel's party had indeed exaggerated his embarrassments, but they were sufficiently heavy. Returning unable to fulfil his undertaking to his creditors, he should awaken a hundred sinister suspicions. The fire would be but a bad excuse for the delay, where all excuses prolonged the chapter of accidents. So Melcomb dreaded to make his appearance until everything was definitively arranged, and he could meet his foes with renewed promises of satisfaction.

To his unsuspected rival the fire was a godsend. It sent his patroness to London, exactly when with a doubting heart, Sinson was preparing to visit her in Cornwall, and thus enabled him to hold down his bondman Everope, with one hand, while with the other he preferred his audacious suit. Could Mrs. Pendarrel have read what was passing in her servant's heart, when he came cringing before her with congratulations on the result of the trial and condolence for the ruin of her house mingled in equal proportions, she would have cursed the hour when she took the fawning rustic into her service. He was now manœuvring to induce the wretched Everope to go abroad, in order that his last fears might be laid to sleep. But the spendthrift was not at all willing to accede to the proposition. And after all, Sinson thought, what did it matter? A little space would disclose the whole of his plot. And when his patroness was once implicated, there would be no danger of exposure. Should circumstances make it necessary, the Trevethlans might be quietly re-instated in their small patrimony, and Michael would be perfectly contented with the domain of Pendarrel. Everope might do as he pleased.

And now Esther had the mortification—for such it was to her—of receiving condolence from all the circle of her acquaintance. The burning of her house made no little stir in the metropolis. In public it was not unreasonably mentioned as affording a good ground for the general alarm. It might figure considerably in the Parliamentary debates—we need not specify the volume of Hansard—it might occupy some space in the reports of secret committees; it might have a green bag all to itself. It was the topic of the day, and became a source of so much exasperation to the mistress of the ruined mansion, that she would almost have rejoiced to sink Pendarrel in some fathomless pool off the Lizard. It is so difficult to condole in a manner at all sufferable. Rarely is it pleasant to be pitied. People are apt to lavish their sorrow on what they think they would have most regretted themselves, and to forget the real weight of the calamity, in considering some detail which strikes their particular fancy. So Angelina might remember the gold fish in the garden, and hope they were not killed when the water was needed for the engines. Now as Esther really loved her home, and deeply deplored its ruin, it sometimes cost her an effort to answer her friends' sympathy with polite equanimity. For the condolers mean kindly, and must be kindly met.

But she was gratified also at times. Some hardy spirit would venture to approach her with a sarcasm. The town, that is to say such men as Winesour, could recollect the late Mr. Trevethlan, at the time he was squandering his fortune; when his companions called him a fool, and were very fond of his society. Such people remembered him with a certain kind of attachment, and heard of the final ruin of his supposed children with a certain sort of regret. And some of them were half aware of the old love-passages between the lord of the castle and the lady of the hall, and guessed for themselves the cause of Henry Trevethlan's desperation. And so with polished incivility, they contrived to compare the fire and the law-suit, and to send a diamond-headed shaft home to Mrs. Pendarrel's heart.

Now this Esther liked. It exasperated her, but it put her upon her mettle; and enabled her to exhibit a wit, delicate and keen as any that attacked her. And she wanted something of the kind. Disguise it as she would, she was bitterly humiliated by the catastrophe of that terrible night.

"Pendar'l and Trevethlan would own one name,"

when there was no place of the former appellation to claim its share in the prediction. The prophecy itself seemed to mock her. The fretfulness induced by these conflicting emotions, restrained abroad, vented itself at home, and fell heavily upon poor Mildred.

And now London was very full. The brilliant froth was bubbling and foaming over the edges of the cup. And so a perpetual round of gaiety invited the votaries of fashion, like the whirling dance about the funeral pyre of Arvalan. Into the fascinating circle Mrs. Pendarrel led her daughter, and took pains to let every one know, that the fillet was already bound round the victim's brow.

But the latter was as little likely to succumb in patience to the intended doom, as the German poet's Bride of Corinth.

And was Esther at all mindful of her defeated adversaries? She heard of their answering her trembling invitation by a precipitate abandonment of their ancient home, and she took little heed of their further proceedings. She did not yet know the full extent of her triumph, and left the effects of the verdict to be developed in the dens of the lawyers.

CHAPTER IV.

O Primavera, gioventù del' anno,
Bella madre de' fiori,
D'erbe novelle, e di novelli amori,
Tu torni ben, ma teco
Non tornano i sereni
E fortunati di delle mie gioje:
Tu torni ben, tu torni,
Ma teco altro non torna,
Che del perduto mio caro tesoro
La rimembranza misera e dolente.

GUARINI.

Spring and Favonius were rapidly loosening the bonds of winter, when Randolph and his sister returned to their old quarters at Hampstead, with feelings very different from those which had attended their first arrival there. Six months had revolutionized their existence. And when in the tumult of emotion which followed the trial at Bodmin, the disinherited heir conceived the idea of seeking the roof which had sheltered his brief studentship, it was rather in that mockery with which despair often tries to delude itself, than with a serious purpose of fulfilling the design. He cast a sneering and scornful glance upon his sojourn in London, and thought of resuming it as a bitter jest. But come what might, he was resolved to quit Trevethlan, and that instantly. Where then could he go? Where find a home for Helen?—questions which Randolph answered by accepting in earnest the plan which he had conceived in irony. Let their old host and hostess enjoy a nine days' wonder.

So to Hampstead the orphans went, making a more leisurely journey than before, and arriving, free from fatigue, in the evening. They were received with warm cordiality.

"What!" said Peach to Randolph, when Helen had retired, "you slept last night at Basingstoke! Not disturbed, I hope, by any of the monk of Croyland's adversaries. Hear Fœlix concerning the foes of monastic rest, as Camden reports his very middling hexameters—

'Sunt aliqui quibus est crinis rigidus, caput amplum,
Frons cornuta, gena distorta, pupilla coruscans,
Os patulum, labra turgentia, dens peracutus—

Nonnulli quibus est non horrida forma, sed ipse
Horror, cum non sint scelerati, sed scelus ipsum.'"

Cornelius loved to hear himself talk, and this was a favourite quotation with him. Randolph assured him the inn at Basingstoke was quite free from the plagues of Croyland Abbey. And then, in a few brief sentences he acquainted Mr. Peach with his real quality. His landlord was amused with the romance.

"Why," said he, "you are like my Lord Burleigh, wooing his peasant-love under the guise of a painter."

A short time before, the remark would have occasioned a severe twinge, but now there was no room for any. Randolph was surrounded by a sea of troubles, and knew not in which direction to strike. And the full effect of the verdict was as yet unperceived by him. He had not observed that by dissolving all ties between himself and his father, it would deprive him not merely of his real estate, the castle and its precincts, but also of all the personal property which he possessed in the world. The next of kin would follow the heir-at-law. In this case they were combined in the same person. Would any mercy be shown? Would it be accepted if it were? The orphans were literally beggars. Nay, they were even in debt. For a rigorous account might be exacted of every farthing of property, which the late Mr. Trevethlan left behind him at his death. And thus opprobium, immediate and inevitable, was hanging over Randolph's head.

The lawyers, of course, were well aware of this. But Mr. Truby, about whom there was nothing of the pettifogger, was in no hurry to advise his client to rush to extremities. He remembered the judge's observation at the trial, that additional evidence would probably be forthcoming before very long, and was not anxious to bear on the defeated party, in a manner which might afterwards be termed oppressive. He always hated sharp practice. He felt bound to mention the state of the case to Mr. Pendarrel, and that gentleman of course communicated it to his wife. Esther started at the news, but perceiving that every day would only involve the orphans more deeply, she was contented to let her advantage rest for a while.

On the other hand, Mr. Winter did not feel it on any account necessary to point out his real position to Randolph. Being certain that injustice had been done, although at present unable to see his way to its reversal, he was loth to risk the disclosure to one of so passionate and obstinate a temper as his client. And in truth the latter's condition required no aggravation. Randolph was in the plight, most harassing to a hot and impatient mood, when there is nothing immediately to be done, and the spirit chafes and rages at its forced inertness.

He sought his friend and counsel, Rereworth, but without obtaining any consolatory information. Seymour was endeavouring to trace the witness whose testimony had overthrown his friend. But hitherto wholly without success. Everope had disappeared entirely from all his former haunts. His chambers were perpetually closed, and the old woman, who acted as his laundress, knew nothing at all concerning her master's movements. Yet this was the quest which Rereworth thought held out the best hope of success; for if the spendthrift's evidence were bought, there were many circumstances conceivable, under which he might be induced to confess.

Very few days had elapsed after the arrival of the orphans at Hampstead, when they were joined by Polydore Riches. He brought them all the details of the conflagration at Pendarrel. And with wrath and indignation Randolph learned that it was pretty generally regarded in the country as a reprisal for the verdict at Bodmin. Not such was the retaliation he desired. The chaplain also grieved his old pupils with an account of the numerous arrests which had been made among the dependents of the castle. It seemed as though their own ruin involved that of many besides.

There was another circumstance connected with this intelligence which was of deep interest to Randolph. The Pendarrels had returned to London. He again breathed the same air with Mildred. Now he had almost rejoiced in the idea that this would not be the case. He was glad that in the dreary interval devoted to the recovery of his rights, during which he had vowed to see her no more, distance would remove any temptation to break the resolution. But she was again within his reach. Any day, in walking through the streets of the metropolis, she might cross his path. He would be in continual expectation of such a meeting. An instant might overthrow all his determination. It was another element to mingle in the turbulence of his emotions.

And the chaplain bore a missive also, which was a source of considerable discussion; namely, Mrs. Winston's letter to Helen, containing the invitation to her house. Gertrude had written with great tact, and with a full consciousness of the delicacy which might revolt from accepting an obligation from the daughter of Esther Pendarrel. She went so far as to say that her offer would probably be disagreeable to her mother if it were known, but she hoped to prevent that, until some fortunate discovery had re-instated her cousins in their just rights. And she infused into her whole letter a warmth of kindness and sympathy which she trusted would not be without its effect. For in truth she wrote from her heart.

But the proposal led to great demur. Randolph abhorred the idea of accepting anything like favour from any of his enemy's house; and was not disposed to admit Mrs. Winston's view of her independence. Yet, being married, she might be considered as no longer involved in the quarrel. And

Randolph was very anxious to find his sister a home. She was in his way. He felt it with no want of affection. But whenever in his reveries he looked forward to the career he should adopt, as soon as he had re-established the good fame of his family, his sister always recurred to his mind as an obstacle in his path. Sketching for himself an adventurous course in some far-distant land, he was always recalled from the vision by the thought of her he should in such case be compelled to leave unprotected, behind. A very short glimpse into the future would have spared him much fruitless speculation.

Helen, with that gentle longing for a reconciliation which she showed in the very opening of this narrative, read Mrs. Winston's letter with pleasure, and desired to accept the invitation. In answer to her brother's peevish dissatisfaction, she urged that her visit might be very short, but that it would be ungrateful, uncharitable, every way perverse, to reject what was offered with such true kindness. She should be entirely private,—should, of course, hold no intercourse with Mr. or Mrs. Pendarrel, and could see Randolph as often and as freely as he pleased.

The chaplain supported Helen's argument with all his power. And in the end the brother yielded, little thinking to what a train of circumstances the visit would give rise. And so Miss Trevethlan removed to Cavendish-square, where Gertrude's winning demeanour soon put her completely at her ease, and where she walked through those same rooms, in which she might remember that Randolph encountered Mrs. Pendarrel face to face, and made the avowal which cut short his career as a student of the law.

He himself escorted her, and quivered a little as he stood in the well-remembered drawing-room. But he only staid a few minutes before returning to Hampstead, through the long and squalid suburb which then lay at the foot of the hill. The stuccoed terraces of the Regent's-park were still in the brain or the portfolio of the architect. The realization of Darwin's prophecy,

"Soon shall thy arm, unconquered Steam, afar
Drag the slow barge, or drive the rapid car,"

although it had taken place on one element, seemed as far distant on shore as when the poet wrote. What wonders have been wrought in these thirty years of peace! And is it possible to think, that once more our progress may be arrested by war, and that the energies which have so long been devoted to the cause of civilization—that great cause of the whole human race, in which nations may fraternize without reciprocal encroachment, which is identical with the advance of true liberty, and of the only equality which mortals can attain, that of virtue—is it possible that these energies can once more be required for self-defence, that the death-drum may again summon us to repel a foreign foe, or that symbols and watchwords may divide ourselves, and our ancient flag find a rival standard unfurled by the sons of those who fought the battle of freedom? Rather let us hope that the convulsions around us may be found to have cleared the air, and brought the day more near,

"When the drum shall throb no longer, and the battle-flag be furled,In the parliament of man, the federation of the world."

The coming of Polydore Riches was an event of some interest to the worthy couple of the peachery. Clotilda, in common with most spinsters of her age, was much in the habit of criticising the mien and aspect of clergymen, and formed her own idea of the appearance of the chaplain from the respect and affection with which Helen always spoke of him. And it must be owned she was a little disappointed. She had expected rather a portly man, with white hair, and a commanding presence. She encountered a slight figure and a pale face, the habitual pensiveness of which was now deepened by anxiety, and which was shaded by locks wherein silver had as yet but little share. Miss Peach allowed that Polydore was "interesting," but she had expected something more.

But Randolph was quite right in predicting that the chaplain and Cornelius would agree together admirably. The two old bachelors speedily conceived a high mutual esteem. Their tastes were very similar. In each there was the same simplicity of character. Polydore was more refined and enthusiastic; Cornelius more humorous and practical. The worthy host soon prevailed on his new friend to join him in a pipe, a luxury in which the chaplain had scarcely indulged since he quitted the classic shades of Granta. And they exhaled the fragrant fumes, due to Peach's ancient friend Sir Walter, so long, that the old clerk fell into a rhapsody on the perfections of that creature of his dreams, Mabel; and actually extracted from Polydore a murmured panegyric on that treasure of his memory, Rose Griffith. And then might a spectator have been amused to observe how the names of Mabel and Rose alternated with the puffs of smoke, and were often sighed forth in concert, with a pathos that might have done honour to the unworthily-used Malvolio.

CHAPTER V.

Margaret. To me what's title when content is wanting?
Or wealth, raked up together with much care,
And to be kept with more, when the heart pines,
In being dispossessed of what it longs for
Beyond the Indian mines? Or the smooth brow
Of a pleased sire, that slaves me to his will,
Leaving my soul nor faculties nor power
To make her own election?

Allworth. But the dangersThat follow the repulse,——

Margaret. To me they're nothing:Let Allworth love, I cannot be unhappy.

MASSINGER.

As Mr. Winston's suggestion to his wife, that she should ask Miss Trevethlan to their house, seemed suddenly to improve their mutual understanding, so did Helen's acceptance of the invitation make them still better known to each other. Among the commonest and worst features of unions like theirs, is a prejudice on one side or the other that happiness is impossible, which closes every avenue to amelioration. The discontented parties have eyes only for defects. The heart which accepted the match with ill-disguised repugnance, is subsequently too proud to admit it was in error. It will not resign the privilege of complaint. It insists on continually galling itself with what it calls its chains. It hugs the satisfaction of considering itself ill-used. For the world, it would not allow itself, even in reverie, to be at ease. Yet, when there is no real deficiency either in character or temper, a hopeful spirit will probably soon find grounds for esteem, and esteem will be likely to ripen into affection. And then the very contrasts of disposition which at first appeared to preclude sympathy, will really promote it, by furnishing opportunities for good-humoured mirth, instead of objects for silent peevishness.

Gertrude Winston had never thought it worth her while to understand her husband. She married him as a pure negation, preferring King Log to King Stork. He was neither sulky, nor mean, nor selfish; he was not meddlesome, nor fidgety, nor exacting. His wife never heard a sharp word from his lips. Surely she might have taken the trouble to go a little below the surface, and see if his pedantry and apathy concealed no qualities which she might first admire, and then love. But no; she had determined to be a "victim," and resolutely closed both heart and mind against any appreciation of whatever might be endearing in his disposition. And for him,—indolent and even-tempered, having married because people usually married, in the same way as they were born and buried,—he certainly took no pains to display his merits, and allowed his wife to do exactly as she pleased, without let or hinderance.

And Gertrude did not abuse the licence. She would not have asked Helen to her house without consulting her husband. In his ready though measured proposal to that effect, Mrs. Winston felt there was a kindness which she had failed to perceive in all his previous demeanour towards her. And when their guest arrived, he surprised her still more by rousing himself from his monotonous pursuits to find sources of interest and amusement for Miss Trevethlan. Gertrude was far above jealousy, and attributed his attentions to their true motive,—a desire to alleviate the anxiety of their new friend.

Yet was Helen one who might well awaken the domestic fiend. Rather under the average height of woman, but of a full and luxurious form, she moved with that soft and undulating mien which fascinates even from afar; and if, allured by the figure, you permitted yourself to advance and look upon the face, you would find it was worthy of the shape. You would see a forehead of the purest white, not very high, but broad and serene, shaded by long dark ringlets, and supported by eyebrows of the same colour, rather far apart, and very slightly arched. Under these you would look into eyes also as dark as night, so gentle and so fond, that well would it be for you if they did not haunt your slumbers for many a night to come. Their long lashes drooped over cheeks perhaps a thought too pale, but so transparently fair that they flushed with every transient emotion, and then almost rivalled the full and tempting lips, which lost themselves in dimples at each corner, and showed that the pensiveness usually characterizing the countenance was not unwilling to give place to any gaiety of the hour.

At the present time, however, pensiveness prevailed, and increased the contrast which Helen's beauty always presented to the attractions of her cousins. She might trace in Mrs. Winston a strong resemblance to the features of the miniature found upon her father's heart, which she had since worn upon hers, and whose original she detected at that eventful visit to the opera. There were the same inscrutable dark eyes, like those in which Charles Lamb said lurked the depth of Jael; there were the same haughty will, and the same decision of purpose; but there was, Helen thought, something more of tenderness and less of disdain.

She had been but a very short time in Cavendish-square when she made the acquaintance of Mildred. Having informed her sister of her invitation, Mrs. Winston could scarcely avoid the introduction, although she was cognizant of a certain secret. Helen possessed no corresponding knowledge, yet a gentle confidence grew up between the maidens, and Mildred perhaps regarded her cousin as not unlikely to be more nearly related to her. Naturally also, and unavoidably, she heard not a little concerning Randolph, and listened to such intelligence with no untroubled heart.

Indeed she had begun to think of him more than was prudent; forced into the recollection by her situation at home. She saw that Mrs. Pendarrel was daily proceeding in the same course she had adopted in Cornwall, and that she herself was becoming more and more involved in conduct which she loathed. She found it very difficult to procure an explanation with her mother, for since the short colloquy in which she attempted to remonstrate the morning after the country party, Mrs. Pendarrel had abruptly checked all further efforts of the same sort. At length, half in despair, Mildred thought of appealing, perhaps for the first time in her life, to her father.

It was a very poor prospect. The scheming younger brother had long sunk into the intriguing political hack. Obsequious, cold, worldly-minded, and correct, was Mr. Trevethlan Pendarrel. He would as soon have thought of absenting himself from a division, as of interfering with his wife's domestic rule. He dared not even object to her lavish expenditure, although he was fonder of money than of anything else; and he was too dull a plodder in official harness to understand the jests sometimes made at his expense. He was greatly surprised when his daughter intercepted him one day on his return home, and led him into a parlour.

"Papa," Mildred said, "I am sure you love me."

"Of course, of course," he answered. "But your mamma takes care of all that." He thought she was going to ask for money.

"But pray do hear me, papa. They say ... This marriage...."

"Of course, my dear. Your mamma has arranged it all. Very agreeable man, Mr. Melcomb. Calls me Petruchio. Marriage! Why, you'll be the envy of half the ladies in London!"

"But, papa, it cannot be. I have told him so."

"Cannot! I don't understand. You must speak to mamma. She manages it all. There—there—"

So saying, he kissed her cheek hastily and departed. Mildred knew not where to turn. Her mother's tactics defeated the support which she had expected from Mrs. Winston, for although the latter threw all the discredit she could upon the rumours of the approaching marriage, no pretence was afforded for any interference of a more active kind. But Mildred, becoming more and more restless, at length seized an opportunity of telling her mother suddenly, that she would go no more into society until the report of her engagement was positively contradicted. Mrs. Pendarrel flew into a violent rage. All her plans were very far advanced. Almost every particular was definitely settled. She was flushed with her triumph at Bodmin. Was everything to be undone by the whim of a foolish girl?

"What!" Esther exclaimed, with fury sparkling in her eyes, "have you courage to be openly disobedient? Will you dare to fly in my face? Do you think to make me wanting to my pledged word? Do you imagine I will bear the scoffs and taunts bestowed upon a beaten match-maker? No, Miss Pendarrel. You will marry as I bid you, or—but there is no alternative."

In the heat of her anger, Esther almost gasped for breath. She had for some time observed her daughter's manner with smouldering wrath, and now Mildred's avowal produced a fierce burst of flame. It deprived Mrs. Pendarrel of her prudence.

"And hark!" she cried. "Do you suppose that I am blind? Do you fancy I know nothing about what you call your heart? Have I forgotten who trembled on my arm, when that upstart pretender dared to intrude into society which he could not have entered honestly, and laid claim to a name to which he had no right? Do I not remember whose cheeks were reddened, and whose voice said 'my cousin?'"

Mildred's cheeks were red enough now, and she trembled from head to foot, and opened her lips to speak, but her mother continued with increasing vehemence.

"And suppose he had been Randolph Trevethlan, as he falsely called himself; suppose that he had been a true descendant of that ancient house, and lawful owner of Trevethlan Castle, do you dream, girl, that I would suffer his alliance with a daughter of mine? Do you not know that I hate him? Do you not know that he hates me? Did I not hunt his father to death? Have I not pursued him, the son of that base peasant-woman, with a hatred which can only be extinguished in the grave? Have I not even now consummated his ruin? Has he a house to hide his head? Is he not a beggar on the earth?"

Again Mrs. Pendarrel paused for breath. Mildred's colour came and went with agitation, and she panted as if her heart would break. She had not in the least expected to arouse such a storm.

"And this is the miserable person you have dared to love? Yes; I ask you again, do you think I am blind, or that there are no eyes but mine? Did I not hear of that meeting on the cliff? Of folding arms, and hands clasped, and lips——? Ay, girl, do you quiver and blush? Cousin, indeed! A creature that has no right to any name at all; homeless, houseless, penniless! Do you know that he is at this moment in my hands? that I can throw him into prison, to languish till he dies? And where is he? where is he hiding? Do you know that his people are charged with the burning of Pendarrel, that he may be implicated himself? Fie, girl! Shall the lion love the jackal? Shall the eagle love the owl?"

"Mother," Mildred ejaculated, taking advantage of another break in Esther's fierce harangue, "I love Randolph Trevethlan! I have vowed to be his wife; and I will."

She was leaving the room, but Mrs. Pendarrel caught her by the wrist and detained her, looking full in her face, and almost choking with the rage which she was unable to express.

"Yes, mother," Mildred said, faltering as she spoke, "in that meeting, which was watched by some miserable spy—that meeting, which I shall remember for ever, which brings no shame to my cheek—in that meeting Randolph won the pledge which nothing but death can break. Did I love him when first I called him my cousin? Did I love him at that meeting on the cliff? Mother, I love him now a thousandfold. Is he houseless, homeless, an outcast, and a beggar? The more need has he of my love. Tell me not of dishonour: there is none with him. Speak to me not of shame: I know it not with him. Is his fate in your hands? So is mine. They cannot be divided. He is mine, and I am his."

As her daughter spoke, Mrs. Pendarrel tightened her hold upon her wrist, and when she flung it loose at the close of Mildred's words, it was discoloured by the pressure. She flung it scornfully from her, and said, in tones whose concentrated but cold indignation was remarkably at variance with her previous vehemence:—

"Go to your chamber, girl. We must see a quick end to this folly. And as for him, you have sealed his doom."

Mildred obeyed, and retired to her own apartment. There she threw herself on a couch, and wept long and passionately. But one thought at last seized her, and restored her to herself.

"His doom sealed!" she murmured. "Did my mother say his doom was sealed? And through me? No, no: it must not be. And is he, indeed, in such danger and distress, and I here, far away, instead of sharing his sorrows, as is my right and my duty? Oh, mother! mother! you little know what you have done."

And she rose, and dried her eyes, and wrote two notes, inclosing one within the other, and directing the outer one to Helen Trevethlan. She had never been one of those dramatic heroines who, in every little trouble, seek consolation from their maids. With regard to them, one might be inclined to avail oneself of the qualification attached to the Highgate oath. Mildred had never asked Rhoda to do her any secret service before. But when she summoned her now, and requested her to convey the note she had just written to its destination at Mrs. Winston's, the natural quickness of a soubrette at once perceived, from the mere selection of the messenger, that the errand was confidential, and it was with gratified self-esteem that Rhoda accepted the mission, and delivered the billet into Miss Trevethlan's own hands. Rhoda advanced very rapidly in the confidence of her young mistress that evening.

Mrs. Pendarrel had been thunderstruck by the attitude assumed by her daughter. She had wrapped herself securely in reliance upon her own power, and so bold a defiance almost stunned her. She bitterly regretted the sarcasms into which she had been betrayed by passion. She readily perceived the effect they would have upon a temper like Mildred's, a temper in some respects like her own. And should all her schemes, all the plans which she built up with so much care and labour, be frustrated by the obstinacy of a love-sick girl? Should Esther Pendarrel confess herself defeated? There was little hope of that. But she felt dim fears and doubts besetting her. She experienced anew some of the despondency caused by the destruction of her house; she looked to the future with some foreboding of evil. But activity must subdue all such misgivings. This insolent suitor must be crushed at once. Her daughter must be schooled into instant submission. Nearly cotemporaneously with Mildred's letter-writing, her mother also indited two epistles. The one she despatched the same evening, by a trusty hand, to Tolpeden Park; the other she sent immediately to Messrs. Truby's offices in Lincoln's Inn.

There would apparently be some searing of hearts, before the war which was that day proclaimed arrived at a peaceful termination.

CHAPTER VI.

These violent delights have violent ends,
And in their triumph die; like fire and powder,
Which, as they kiss, consume. The sweetest honey
Is loathsome in its own deliciousness,
And in the taste confounds the appetite:
Therefore, love moderately; long love doth so;
Too swift arrives as tardy as too slow.

SHAKSPEARE.

It was a notable fact at this time that Seymour Rereworth, the recluse law-student, whom Mrs. Winston used to rally for his devotion to so crabbed a mistress, became a frequent haunter of the house in Cavendish Square. His acquaintance with the Trevethlans, and his relationship to Gertrude, opened the door, closed to all besides, of that little boudoir where she and Helen used to sit together, when they were unengaged; precisely the same room from which Randolph pointed out to Mildred the star which he fancifully chose as the arbiter of his destiny. There Rereworth, forsaking the tangled intricacies of Astræa, learned to disentangle skeins of silk; there, instead of threading the mazes of some perplexing quibble, he could, on occasion, thread a needle; there, instead of reading of the wars of the alphabet, A against B, and C against D, he would read aloud the newest poem of Byron, or the latest novel of Scott; and Seymour was a good reader, and did not object to hear himself read, particularly when Helen Trevethlan listened. And the expression one can throw into such poetry and such prose is very convenient. So Rereworth was now the Corsair, with—

My own Medora, sure thy song is sad.

Then Selim, with—

Bound where thou wilt, my barb; or glide, my prow—But be the star that guides the wanderer—thou.

And again he played the romantic with Flora Mac Ivor, or sang serenades with Henry Bertram. It is, we say, a convenient way of making love, which was something very like Seymour's present occupation, when—

The deep, the low, the pleading tone
With which we *read* another's love,
Interpret may our own.

Pleasant it is to contrast the even and tranquil affection which was thus ripening between Rereworth and Miss Trevethlan, with the turbulent and rebellious passion which linked together Mildred and Randolph. Helen had soon learned to like her brother's friend in his winter visits to Mr. Peach's cottage: her heart thanked him for the zeal which he now displayed in investigating the fraud practised at the recent trial; and she listened to these readings in a mood prepared readily to acquiesce in the emotions they were calculated to excite. Although it must be confessed that the wild passions of Lord Byron's heroes had more in common with the angry humour of Randolph than with her own gentle disposition. Perhaps her pleasure was derived from the voice of the reader rather than the poetry which he read.

But Rereworth did not allow his attentions to the sister to prevail over his exertions on behalf of the brother. And Randolph, being now more independent, seconded his friend's efforts with his own. But it was a vague and unsatisfactory pursuit. With no little difficulty they opened a correspondence with the family of Everope, but they were disappointed in its result; for nothing precise could be recollected respecting the spendthrift's movements in that eventful autumn. His connections were by no means anxious to revive their knowledge of his habits. And in London he seemed to have entirely abandoned all his former haunts. His chambers remained permanently closed; no one had seen him for a long time. Restless and impatient, Randolph roamed through the metropolis, scrutinizing the wayfarers, until his eyes became weary of the endless succession of unknown faces. Occasionally he visited places of questionable resort, having learned that such were much frequented by the object of his chase. Thus, once or twice, he went to the Argyll Rooms, and walked, care-worn and sad, among the giddy throng, where most especially, even in laughter, the heart was sorrowful, and the end of mirth was heaviness. And there one night he was mocked with a glimpse of the man he sought. He was watching, partly with interest, and partly with aversion, the proceedings at the hazard-table, when he noticed a player sitting opposite him, the quivering of whose fingers, as his forehead rested on them, showed how keen was his anxiety in the game. While Randolph was observing him, a showy woman laid her hand upon the gambler's shoulder, and made him look up with a start. At the same moment his eye met Randolph's; he saw he was recognised, rose and vanished; and though his pursuer hurried after him, his inexperience and want of acquaintance with the ways of the place enabled Everope to elude his search.

Meantime, at Trevethlan, Griffith was quietly following another trail. He took the proceedings at the inquest on the supposed Ashton as the basis of his hopes, and was eagerly inquiring among the country people what was remembered of the occurrences on the night of his suspected murder; for it might be presumed that they could not now feel any reluctance to tell all they knew, as the lapse of time would be sufficient to save them from harm. And, accordingly, the steward had little difficulty in ascertaining the particulars of the smuggling adventure of the night in question, and found that it was generally supposed the murderer had escaped in the lugger which came in with the illicit cargo. But there his researches were brought to an end. What had become of that lugger? In what seas she had sailed since, over what parts of the globe her crew were dispersed, were questions more easily asked than answered, with respect to a vessel of her character.

The hamlet was plunged in mourning. Already the note of preparation had been sounded for the formal taking possession of the castle by its new proprietor, and no rescue seemed probable. The old prediction was to be fulfilled at the expense of Trevethlan. The evil omen of the late squire's marriage was to be borne out by the event. And not a few families in the village were still bewailing the absence of some member now imprisoned on a charge of being concerned in the outrage at Pendarrel. The utmost rigour of the law was threatened against the guilty, and the offence was capital. The dark hour which old Maud Basset said was at hand for the house of Trevethlan had indeed arrived, and gloom hung around the towers on the cliff, and over the green of the hamlet.

The wrath of the villagers ran high against all who had in any way abetted the law-suit, and in particular against Michael Sinson. Upon his head many an imprecation was breathed, and against him many a threat was muttered. And the odium reflected upon his sweetheart. The people abused her for her rejection of Edward Owen. They said it was due to her that he was now lying in jail. They pointed at her, and flouted her. And poor Mercy often thought of the dismal denunciations of Dame Gudhan, and shuddered at the idea they might prove true.

Old Maud also shared in the unpopularity of her grandson. Over and over again the folks dinned into her ears that Margaret's marriage was broken, and that it was all her Michael's doing. That was the reason, they said, that the castle and lands passed away from Squire Randolph. It was her own favourite that had brought shame on the daughter of whom she was so proud. But Maud refused to understand. She sat, hour after hour, swaying herself to and fro in her rocking-chair, exulting in the ruin of the family which had wronged her Margaret, and, in a low voice, murmuring the hymns she had learned in childhood.

It would seem the fortunes of that family could hardly sink lower, but such was not the case. Griffith received a letter from Winter, informing him that Mr. Pendarrel's lawyer had intimated he was instructed to demand a rigid account of all the personal property left by his late master, and that, although he had replied the demand would be resisted, still the steward had better prepare for the worst. As yet no light appeared to brighten the condition in which they were left by the verdict in the ejectment. Griffith lifted up his hands in tribulation, and looked back through those five-and-thirty years.

This announcement was the result of Mrs. Pendarrel's interview with Mr. Truby. She insisted on the lawyer pressing all the legal consequences of the verdict to the utmost, and without delay. She even inquired whether the so-called Mr. Trevethlan might not be arrested. But Truby coldly answered, that though perhaps he might, yet he could not be detained, and that such a procedure would be at variance with the common courtesy. Common courtesy! Mrs. Pendarrel might think, what courtesy is there between me and him? She did not, however, venture to urge her proposition further.

But we are anticipating a little. Randolph remained unaware of this new device to drive him to utter ruin. One evening, after a day spent in the fruitless wanderings which occupied so much of his time, he was sitting with Polydore Riches, silent and languid, thinking moodily of abandoning all hope, and at once proceeding to some distant land in quest of enterprise— South America seemed to offer a field—when the post brought him a letter. He saw it was from Helen, and opened it slowly and without much curiosity. But it contained an enclosure, addressed to himself, in a lady's writing with which he was unacquainted. That he unfolded with more despatch, and read:—

> "Randolph—I am yours. I must see you. Meet me to-morrow afternoon, at three, near the keeper's lodge, in Kensington-gardens.—Your——
>
> "M. P."

The blood rushed into the reader's pallid cheeks. The very encounter which he had at times dreaded, while threading his way through the crowded streets, was here pressed upon him in a manner which he could not elude. Would he wish, then, to avoid it? Perhaps not. But in the first confusion of his feelings, joy had only a small share. Again all his plans were frustrated. He seemed to be a mere plaything in the hands of destiny.

It wanted yet some time of the appointed hour when the lover sought the rendezvous. Backwards and forwards, with uneven steps, he paced the grass between the cottage and the Serpentine-river. The thought of avenging the desolation around him again presented itself to his fancy: again he resisted it, and vowed that no such selfish impulse should sully his affection for Mildred. But the idea recalled the death-bed injunctions of his father, and reminded him that he had been on the point of entirely submitting to his adversary's triumph. He began to think that the task which had been imposed upon him was beyond his strength. His dreamy and lonely youth had ill prepared him for the storms of riper years. He was infirm of purpose and irresolute of heart.

The approach of a female form fluttered his pulse, and in a moment he was at Mildred's side. The greeting was incoherent and abrupt.

"Randolph," the lady said, "I have sought you, because I have no other succour left. Do you know, have they told you, that my bridal is at hand?"

Her lover started, and remembered, as in a flash of lightning, what he had heard from old Jeffrey.

"It was false," he said. "Dearest, I knew it was false."

"Ay," she continued. "But it has become very like truth. Do you know that everybody believes it? that everybody looks upon Mildred Pendarrel.... Oh, my mother, my mother, why have you driven me to this?"

She spoke with passionate sorrowfulness of accent. Well might Randolph say there was no happiness in love like theirs.

"Yes, the day is fixed. I am a prisoner till it comes. I am here only by stealth. I do not know what will become of me. I can bear it no longer."

The words followed one another in rapid succession. Mildred was trying to forget herself in the quickness of her utterance.

"The day will never dawn," Randolph exclaimed. "Are we not vowed to each other? Are we not pledged for ever? Let us fly, dearest. Let us be united before the world, as we are in our hearts. But, no, no," he suddenly ejaculated, with a burst of anguish. "Do you know who I am? An outcast, without house or name. Dishonoured and infamous. What can I offer you? How can you share my lot? It must not be, dearest Mildred, it can never be."

"I know it all," she answered. "It was my mother that pressed it on me. What then? Was it not the very reason that determined me? Oh, Randolph, do not think so lightly of me, as to suppose such things would turn me from my vow. Do not think I would recall what is my only hope, my last-remaining joy. I have nothing left but you. Do not fancy I regret what is gone."

Brief, but earnest and decided, was the conversation that ensued. Passion carried all before it. Mildred thought that, with the help of her faithful Rhoda, she could escape the same evening. Randolph would arrange everything for their flight. The north road would conduct them, if not to happiness, at least to security. A few rapid sentences settled all preliminary details; and the lovers parted, to meet again before many hours were over.

There was now no time for reflection. Randolph had not a minute to spare. There were letters to write for Helen and for Mr. Riches, short as possible, giving, after all, no information. There were funds to provide, little requisites to collect. When Randolph stood by his carriage under the trees of Grosvenor-square, he seemed scarcely to have rested a moment from the time he left Kensington-gardens.

Late in the evening it was. Mildred had retired for the night. Rhoda showed her young mistress, in a slight disguise, to Mrs. Pendarrel's door, as a visitor, and speedily slipped out, unseen, herself. They reached the carriage in safety. The elopement was complete. Scandal laughed in the wind that swept through the trees, as the fugitives were whirled from the square.

CHAPTER VII.

The father was steel, and the mother was stone;
They lifted the latch, and they bid him begone.
But loud on the morrow their wail and their cry!
He had laughed on the lass with his bonny black eye,
And she fled to the forest to hear a love-tale,
And the youth it was told by was Allen-a-Dale.

SCOTT.

The flight was not detected. So when Mrs. Pendarrel descended in the morning to the breakfast room, she was surprised at finding no Mildred there to receive her. She did not at first take much heed to the circumstance, but herself commenced what had usually been her daughter's duty. But when she had been some time joined by her husband, and there were still no signs of the young lady, she desired a servant to send Miss Pendarrel's maid to inquire whether her mistress was not ready for breakfast. Answer came in a few minutes, that Miss Pendarrel's maid was not to be found. Esther then felt some uneasiness; would herself look after the bird; found the cage empty; an incoherent note on the dressing-table:—

"Dearest mother," Mildred briefly wrote, "I can bear it no longer. Every day sinks me deeper in deceit. You do not know—you never can tell, how I have struggled. Why did you upbraid him? Oh, mother, why did you seem to rejoice in his sorrow? I feel that I can only be his. When you know all my despair, you will forgive your child."

"Never," Esther exclaimed, grinding her teeth. She crushed the billet in her hand, and returned to her husband.

"Mr. Trevethlan Pendarrel," said she, "your daughter has eloped."

The politician felt some excitement for once, and blushed like red tape.

"What!" he exclaimed. "What did you say, Esther?"

"Your daughter has eloped, sir," she repeated; "eloped with your pretended nephew. Come, sir; there must be a pursuit."

Roused at last to a sense of the emergency, the bereaved father bestirred himself, obtained some traces of the fugitives, and, within half an hour, was flying along the north road as fast as four horses could take him.

Did any girl ever know the anguish she would inflict by a step like Mildred's? Press to the uttermost the arguments urged by Milton and Johnson in defence of the right of children to choose for themselves in marriage, they will still never be found to countervail the natural sentiments of the heart. They will never subdue conscience, or stifle remorse. And so it has been often observed, that wedlock, in which the honour due to father and mother is forgotten, is rarely happy in its result. And, on the other hand, parents, who, without the most solid grounds, coerce their children's inclinations, will probably one day pay the penalty of their hard-heartedness.

Esther communicated the event in a short and savage note to Mrs. Winston, striving to flatter herself with the idea, that in spite of Mildred's words, she might have sought an asylum in Cavendish-square. Gertrude answered the missive in person, and with great sorrow. She bitterly deplored her sister's imprudence; but Mrs. Pendarrel received her with sharp and angry speech, said what had happened was owing to her teaching, was sorry she had no daughters to serve her in the same way, and, in short, treated her with a contumely which it required all Mrs. Winston's temper to endure in respectful silence.

Esther was almost prostrated by the blow. She had never been quite herself since the burning of Pendarrel. She had, it was true, maintained a bold and haughty front, but she had lost some of her old internal confidence. She had become more hasty, and found her self-control much weakened. She perceived the change in that scene with Mildred, which, as she confessed to herself, had probably hurried the catastrophe more than anything Mrs. Winston had done or said. But when she desired Mildred not to leave the house without her cognizance, she had no idea that the young lady was prepared to disobey.

She read the note of farewell over and over. She crumpled it, and smoothed it, again and again. With all its incoherence, it was sufficiently decided. And so the very same day in which she had fulminated her final decree against the heir of Trevethlan—a decree which she hoped would crush him to the ground—that very day her daughter had thrown herself into his arms. She was check-mated just when she thought the next move would give her the game. Henry Trevethlan was already well avenged.

In the midst of her agitation, word was brought her that Michael Sinson had begged the favour of an audience. She had seen very little of her protégé since her arrival in town. She fancied he might be of some service in her present strait, and granted the permission he sought. Ignorant of Miss Pendarrel's flight, he came cringing into the presence of his patroness, with the idea that Everope was safe, and that he might claim the reward of his treachery.

"Now, sir," his mistress said as he entered, "what is your business with me?"

The young man was embarrassed. He had well considered what he was about to say, yet, when the time came to speak, his words were not ready.

"You know, ma'am," he said, hesitating and confused, "the pains I have taken in exposing the person who had unlawful possession of Trevethlan Castle."

"Well, sir!"

"You know, ma'am, that I did not scruple to bring discredit on some of my own kindred, in order that right might be done."

"You have been well paid," Mrs. Pendarrel said.

"Excuse me, ma'am," Sinson proceeded. "I have been reproached and abused by my relations, and all the country people turn away from me. It is not easy for me to show my face in Kerrier or Penwith. But right is done at last. You have the castle firm and safe. Do you remember, ma'am, what I told you of the late owner and Miss Mildred?"

Esther started, supposing the speaker was going to give her some intelligence respecting the elopement.

"In a week or a fortnight," Michael continued, "there will be no trace of the old family at Trevethlan. The steward is now preparing to quit. Mr. Randolph is wandering somewhere in poverty and want. Do you suppose, ma'am, that he has forgotten that walk on the cliff, with—with your daughter?"

Mrs. Pendarrel was surprised. She could not imagine to what end so strange an introduction was tending. She listened in silence.

"No, ma'am," said her protégé. "Love will not grow cold in ruin."

And then Sinson, in incoherent language, proceeded to contrast Randolph's circumstances with his own. It was a speech which he had often meditated, and spoken in soliloquy, yet he now felt almost unable to deliver it. A sense of the hollowness of his reasoning choked the words which should have flowed from his lips. He was too conscious of his own sophistry to be eloquent. Yet he struggled on through sentence after sentence, without observing the increasing astonishment of Mrs. Pendarrel, who wondered more and more to what he was coming. Like Fear, Michael recoiled from the sound of his own voice, when he had heard his concluding demand.

"Why, then, if this Mr. Randolph is fascinated by—your daughter—why should I be blind to the same attractions?"

By this time Esther had risen from her seat, and stood, mute with amazement. Had Michael been less excited, he could not have failed to notice the scorn and indignation in her face. But he had become absorbed in his subject, and proceeded hurriedly.

"And what obstacle is there? The world's prejudice? That I sweep aside. You can give me what station you please. Her engagement? You have good cause to break it. Why does Melcomb pursue her? To pay off the encumbrances on Tolpeden? No, no: to pay his own debts. Tolpeden will be mortgaged as now. Will she object? Not if she have any regard for Mr. Randolph. I can implicate him in the burning of Pendarrel. His life will be in danger. She will consent, in order to save him. What hinderance is there then?"

Mrs. Pendarrel approached the bell-rope, but before she could pull it, Michael boldly interposed. He had now regained his audacity.

"Hark! ma'am," he said. "Before you venture to scorn this offer, remember what you owe me. I am not to be paid with money. Well paid, did you say? No, ma'am. The triumph you have gained hangs upon my word. A breath from me will blow it to the winds. There is shame in store for you, ma'am, worse than any that has befallen Mr. Randolph. I have letters of yours, ma'am. You are in my power. I have named my terms. Beware, ma'am, of rejecting them."

"You do not seem to be aware, sir," Esther said, with cold and bitter sarcasm, "that the honour you would confer upon my family, it is not in my power to accept. My daughter fled from my house last night, and, as I believe, in company with the person to whom you allude."

"Fled!" Sinson exclaimed in a whisper. "Fled!"

Before he recovered from his astonishment, Mrs. Pendarrel had rung the bell. A servant speedily answered the summons. Michael heard an order which banished him from the house for ever, and stamped fiercely on the floor, while his patroness retired into an adjoining apartment.

"Did you hear, sir?" said the servant tapping Sinson smartly on the shoulder.

An execration rose to the young man's lips, but he repressed it, and followed the attendant. The door of the house closed behind him, and its jar seemed finally to shiver to atoms the fabric he had been constructing so long and so laboriously. He stood on the pavement of the street, once more the vile Cornish peasant. His devices had recoiled upon his own head. One step of a simple girl had disconcerted all his schemes. And he had tied his own hands. But then with a sort of savage glee he thought of the plight of the young lovers. At least he had brought ruin on the house from which he had been driven with disdain. And he retained his hold on Mrs. Pendarrel. He was not lost in loss itself. He must obtain the funds which he had affected to despise. Should he not follow up the idea which he had mentioned of charging Randolph with instigating those incendiaries? There was motive sufficient to make the accusation credible. He could at least tamper with some of those who were in custody. The hope of pardon, the promise of reward would be tempting inducements. He was not yet destitute of resources. And he had the chance of his lottery-ticket.

Such were the notions into which the tumult of Sinson's passions at length subsided. He had gone into the Green Park, and he walked rapidly to and fro, under the trees by Rosamond's Pond. Some people watched him, thinking that he meditated suicide. But his pace became gradually slower and steadier, and the flaneurs went on their way, wondering what might have caused so much agitation.

"No," Michael might have muttered between his teeth; "at least he shall not enjoy any tranquillity. Infamy shall follow poverty. He shall never be happy with her, nor she with him. Let him pay for his father's scornfulness; let her atone for her mother's disdain. Ha! What did I say? What did I betray? But no; I mentioned nothing tangible. No names. No particulars. The secret is safe. Let Mrs. Pendarrel take possession of Trevethlan Castle: she will hold it for me. Let her refuse me my demands, and I blow her title to the winds, and shame her in the sight of the world. And I am safe. There would be nothing against me but what I chose to confess. Ay, the game is not up yet. I shall not have played for nothing. Was I expelled from the castle? Am I driven from the hall? Long shall the heir of the one, and the mistress of the other, rue the contumely they cast upon Michael Sinson."

The muser started, for a hand grasped his arm, and shook him. He looked up, and encountered Everope.

"Do you hear, Sinson?" cried the spendthrift. "Five times I have said your name! What is the matter with you?"

"It's plain enough what is the matter with you," Michael answered moodily. "And why have you not left London? For what are you lingering here? Do you wish to be transported?"

"If I am, you will be also," said Everope. "I must have some money."

Slovenly and jaded, the unhappy man presented obvious signs of recent dissipation. His eyes were bloodshot, and his hand trembled.

"That you may squander it in riot," Sinson said. "Tush! you have had too much already. You think you are worth more than you are. You can only harm yourself. Go abroad, or I shall throw you into the Fleet. Let's see who'll believe your stories there."

"Villain!" exclaimed the spendthrift.

All the fierce and disappointed passions which were struggling in Michael's breast, concurred in giving strength to the blow that sent Everope staggering several paces to fall upon the turf, almost before the word had passed his lips. Sinson turned and walked away.

His bondman rose from the ground in a fury not to be described. All the few traces of the gentleman which still lingered about him, rebelled with hot resentment against the insult he had received. Such are the contradictions of our nature. Mean, profligate, and perjured, Everope yet revolted from a blow. And from whom received? From the tempter to whom he sold himself for a few paltry pieces of gold. From one whom he, even in his own degradation, despised and loathed; who had betrayed him into guilt at which his soul grew sick. And directed against the man who had come to offer him kindness. Yes; how well he remembered that repulsed visit to his chambers in the Temple! With what horror he had recognised his benefactor at the trial! The man whose his testimony had undone had attempted to rescue him from ruin. "Too late it was, too late," Everope cried with his inward voice—"it has always been too late with me. But need it still be so? Was opportunity of retrieval finally gone? Had even the eleventh hour elapsed? Could he not break his chains? It was but to speak one word. The Fleet! There, or worse then there, he must end! Why should he struggle for a few days' respite? What was the wretched timidity which disabled him from facing his position?"

Such was the reverie of him whom want of principle and a sanguine temper had reduced by degrees to the degraded state in which the reader finds him. Always hoping to retrieve the effects of past extravagance, and intending to repair the mischief of former faults, he allowed himself to be led into fresh wastefulness, and to be involved in further guilt. Was his present penitence to be more efficient? The question will soon be answered. He hurried away from the scene of his interview with Sinson, and quitted the park by Buckingham-gate.

Meantime, Michael had not gone very far before a thought seemed to strike him, and he retraced his steps to Rosamond's Pond. After all, it might be prudent not to quarrel with the spendthrift at present. But he was too late. Everope had disappeared. "It is no matter," Sinson muttered; "I can find him at any time." The next day he went down into Cornwall.

"The understanding of a man naturally sanguine"—it is Dr. Johnson who speaks—"may be easily vitiated by the luxurious indulgence of hope, however necessary to the production of everything great or excellent; as some plants are destroyed by too open exposure to that sun which gives life and beauty to the vegetable world."

In Everope is seen the extremity to which the vitiation here mentioned by the great moralist may sometimes be carried. Yet surely a sanguine temperament ought to be a blessing. A willingness to see the bright side of things should not be converted into a misfortune. But it is frequently at once compliant and obstinate, yielding readily to seduction and resisting advice. And it is too often treated in the spirit of the maxim, that wilful men must have their way. That is to say, it is considered to be always in the wrong. A common idea is, that difficulty will cure its faults. But the difficulty must not amount to ruin. The step from the sublime to the ridiculous is not more easy than that from sanguineness to despair.

CHAPTER VIII.

Do you note,
How much her Grace is altered on the sudden?
How long her face is drawn? How pale she looks,
And of an earthly cold? Mark you her eyes?

SHAKSPEARE.

The news of the elopement was of course at first allowed to transpire as little as possible. There was still a faint chance that the errant damsel might be overtaken before she was over the border, in which case the escapade might perhaps be hushed up, and scandal deprived of its prey. But it created anxiety and sorrow at other places besides the house in May-Fair. In Randolph's notes to Helen and to Polydore, he merely said that he was summoned suddenly from town for a few days, and would write again very shortly. He did not dare to entrust the secret of his flight to paper. His communications, therefore, caused great perplexity. It was something quite new for him to show any reserve, towards either the chaplain or his sister. But the mystery was solved by Mrs. Winston, who gently complained that Helen should have availed herself of her visit in Cavendish Square, to become a means of correspondence between the fugitives. She soon saw, however, that Helen's simplicity had alone been to blame, and withdrew her remonstrances.

Polydore was very much disturbed. Was this the end of his teaching? Was it his quiet and meditative pupil, the calm student of the library at Trevethlan, the contemplative muser by the sea, who had thus in one moment flung prudence aside, and fled to an irregular and unhallowed union? The simple-hearted chaplain could not understand it at all. He had sometimes anticipated the pleasure of himself blessing the nuptials of his former pupils, according to the ritual of his church, and now Randolph had contracted a marriage devoid of any ecclesiastical sanction. Improper and ill-omened as had been the father's wedding, that of the son, Mr. Riches thought, was still more deplorable. Such matches were rarely a source of happiness. And here, in particular, the enmity between the families might lead to unusual misery. And poverty—stark, staring poverty—seemed to threaten the young couple. For Polydore had learned from Mr. Winter the last step taken by Mrs. Pendarrel, and saw nothing before the orphans but absolute and immediate want.

And the further letters which before long reached both Helen and the chaplain did not tend to allay their anxiety. Randolph wrote that he and his bride were returning, by easy and leisurely stages, to the metropolis. But there were few traces of happiness, or even of tranquillity in his missives. They contained no spontaneous effusion of joy, no expressions of triumph, no desire for congratulation. They were, on the contrary, cold and restrained. The writer seemed endeavouring to suppress any signs of emotion, to avoid causing uneasiness, to prevent sympathy. Even in speaking of Mildred, he was cautiously reserved. He mentioned her without any warmth of panegyric, and without any overflow of tenderness. Neither did he say a single word in justification of his flight. He seemed to write, rather because he felt bound to do so, than from any pleasure in the correspondence. In fact, Polydore remarked to himself with a sigh, that if Randolph had not wished on his arrival in town to find a temporary abode ready for him where he was not known, he would probably not have written at all. In all this the chaplain saw but slight prospect of future comfort.

Nor was an epistle which Mildred wrote to her sister, although different in tone, more re-assuring. It was much more open and unrestrained, but it exhibited a mood quite as unsatisfactory. The bride strove at great length, and with much passion, to justify her flight. She described in eager and bitter language the long solicitude she had endured, both at Pendarrel Hall and in London. During all that time, she said, she was made to act a lie. She had remonstrated, and implored, and wept. She had been derided, and threatened, and terrified. Her steps had been watched, and at last she had been bidden to consider herself a prisoner. But all this, and more than this, would not have tempted her to fly. It was not until she was told that a certain event was imminent,—it was not until she heard him who was now her husband shamed and calumniated, and declared to be in want and sorrow,— that the idea of consulting with him occurred to her. She had no one to advise her. Gertrude's own promises were too limited. She was distracted. She had no eyes for anything but one immediate and overwhelming danger. Was not *he* on the point of coming from Cornwall? Yet still she did not mean to fly. It was the idea of a moment; hastily adopted, to be executed after an interval too brief to give time for reflection. Were it to be done over again, nothing would induce her to take such a step. She knew all she had forfeited. But she hoped her sister would not judge her too severely. And, finally, she prayed Gertrude to intercede for her with her mother. She should never enjoy a moment's repose until she had obtained her pardon. She acknowledged her undutifulness in terms of the most earnest penitence. Already, she said, her punishment had begun. If it lasted, it would be more than she could bear. Better it would have been to have endured the utmost extremity, than to have incurred her mother's just indignation.

With the arrival of these letters all secresy respecting the affair was at an end. The news spread rapidly from mouth to mouth, that Miss Pendarrel had made a stolen match. The scandal-mongers were gratified to their heart's content. All the details of the flight were discussed with ignorant curiosity;

accidents were invented which had never occurred; and the stratagems by which pursuit was evaded were described with exact inaccuracy.

Border weddings will soon be as legendary as that of Lochinvar. The rail has already destroyed the romance of the journey, and the law will speedily put an end to its profit, by requiring a fortnight's residence before a marriage will be valid. Let "victims," therefore, make haste. It was rather different when Randolph carried off his bride from Grosvenor Square. He had engaged a carriage for the journey, but he wanted time and experience to arrange an express, and was consequently much delayed during the night. The travellers had not accomplished more than fifty miles, when day broke upon them. It had been a silent, though sleepless ride, and morning showed Randolph the traces of tears on Mildred's cheeks. They called to his mind in an instant the extent of the sacrifice she had made; for he would be no party to any suit for reconciliation. He had torn his bride from her station and her friends, and held himself precluded from all attempt to restore her to their love. His father's spirit seemed to whisper in his ear, that for him there could be no communion with those whom Mildred was bound to honour, and whom he had persuaded her to desert. And for what? What lay before himself?

He endeavoured to repel such considerations, and to devote himself to the comforting of his companion. But his efforts were of little avail. He became gloomy and abstracted. So soon did repentance mingle with the feelings of the fugitives. But still they hurried forwards. Retreat, for Randolph at least, was out of the question; and to be overtaken would be defeat. He could afford no such triumph to Philip or Esther Pendarrel. And the father's pursuit was fruitless. He gained upon the chase at every stage; but he came up too late. They were united, never to be put asunder.

They heard of his arrival, and Mildred would have thrown herself at his feet. But her husband would not suffer it. It was rather early for a matrimonial dispute, and a sad occasion of difference. Dark forebodings crowded on the heart of the young wife. It was far from being so that she was bidden to leave father and mother and cleave to her husband. But Randolph would join her in a letter. No; he would not even permit her to write on his behalf. She must strictly confine her apologies to herself. For him, he would make none, and would ask for no forgiveness. It was his part to forgive.

In the sorrow and dismay occasioned by these injunctions, Mildred wrote the letter to her sister which we have sketched above. She gave it to her husband to read. He observed the anguish expressed in every line, and melted into a flood of tenderness, blaming the moodiness of his temper, and praying pardon of his bride. But he said no word which might encourage her to insert a single sentence in his name; and she remembered how, at that meeting on the cliff, Randolph spoke of the hate which was between her mother and himself, and how there could be little of happiness in his love; and the words appeared to be true with a force to bring despair.

With a misgiving heart, Mrs. Winston took her sister's letter to their mother. Esther read it, and gave no sign. She observed that Mildred's entreaties and excuses were confined to herself. There was no mention of her partner in the affront; and Mrs. Pendarrel resented it too fiercely as yet to show any commiseration. Yet she was greatly changed. The successive shocks she had sustained had tamed her haughty resolution. The destruction of her home had caused her many a bitter pang. It was followed by the anxiety and exasperation produced by her daughter's demeanour. These were converted into despondency and fury by the elopement. And then came her miserable agent with a proposal which insulted her, and with menacing hints which were at once a cause of perplexity and alarm. Under such an accumulation of cares, it was no wonder that her old spirit deserted her, and that her usual energy was prostrated.

But no gentle thoughts yet mingled with her dejection. Anger, cold and stern, over-powered every other sentiment. She forgive! She pardon the rebellion which had shattered the hopes of many months! She extend her hand to the man whom she had just driven to ruin! Forego the vengeance which she had meditated for years! Furnish Henry Trevethlan cause to triumph in his grave! Take the child again to her bosom who had wedded a nameless outcast! One whom she, Esther Pendarrel, had just before succeeded in degrading, and whom she could not, if she would, restore! Was it not a fair jest for the world to laugh at? She had disinherited and beggared her foe, only to prepare him to become her daughter's husband. And even now he gave no sign. He was exulting over the check he had put upon her. After all, it was he who had won the game. And should she then forgive?—should she make the victory more complete? No: let them starve;—let them see how poverty and love agreed together. She could at least enjoy that spectacle. And when love grew cold in daily bickerings, when life became a long scene of mutual recrimination, when strife made it happiness to be apart, or guilt brought about an actual separation, then she might think her daughter's penance sufficiently severe, and furnish her with the means of prolonging her miserable existence.

In this dejected and sullen temper Mr. Pendarrel found his wife upon his return from his unsuccessful journey to the north. And he was surprised to discover that he had become of sudden consequence in the household. Esther seemed to have abdicated her rule. She let things take their course with a strange sort of apathy. Her activity vanished, or only showed itself in petty things. She often sat unemployed, and absent of mind for a long time together. She took her husband's advice. But the slightest allusion to the elopement, or any kindred topic, made her eyes gleam in a way to scare the unwary suggester of such a theme. Mr. Pendarrel ventured to hint, soon after his return, at the desirableness of some arrangement, and the reception of the experiment fairly frightened him from repeating it.

It will be remembered that, after the stormy scene with Mildred, Esther despatched a missive to Tolpeden Park. It was to summon its proprietor immediately to town. Melcomb obeyed; and arrived only to learn that his intended bride belonged to another. His career was soon at an end. Embarrassments thickened around him. For some time he played at hide-and-seek with the minions of the sheriff; but at length they triumphed, and Melcomb became an inmate of the King's Bench.

And now he may disappear from these pages. After a while he obtained "the rules;" occupied decent apartments near the Obelisk; joined a club of gentlemen in his own plight, and mimicked on a small scale the habits of a more fortunate time. One evening he was missed from his accustomed tavern. They inquired at his lodgings. He was very ill; and he never rallied. Some of his companions in misfortune consoled his declining hours; and in a few days his heir took joyful possession of Tolpeden.

CHAPTER IX.

None but an author knows an author's cares,
Or fancy's fondness for the child she bears:
Committed once into the public arms,
The baby seems to smile with added charms:
Like something precious ventured far from shore,'
Tis valued for the danger's sake the more.

COWPER.

Polydore Riches, as we have said, was much disturbed by the matrimonial escapade of his old pupil. But his profession, his own experience, and his age, had taught him resignation. It was his favourite theory that things seemed evil only because they were but half seen. Could man discern the whole train of events of which an apparent calamity was part, he would find that what was thought a misfortune was really a blessing. But the eye of reason was as short-sighted as that of the body. There were many things beyond its ken. And, as the most powerful telescopes failed to penetrate beyond a certain distance, and served but to make the vastness of the universe more incomprehensible, so the severest logic only availed to show the limits of the human understanding, and to inspire it with reverent humility for things beyond its bounds. This true and grateful optimism enabled the chaplain to overcome the sharpness of sorrow, and to maintain that unruffled quietude of mind which is the happy mean between apathy and over-susceptibility. Yet, as has been more than once hinted, he was not unacquainted with grief.

He had been into London one day to visit Helen, and also to try to find some of his old college companions, when he met with what was for him a little adventure. It probably led his thoughts into the course shown in a conversation which he held with Mr. Peach the same evening.

"You have several old friends of mine here, Mr. Peach," Polydore said, surveying the row of tall folios which formed his host's library. "Now this is one to whom I was always very partial." And he took down Sir Thomas Browne. "Open this worthy knight where you will, you will be pretty sure to find some intellectual pabulum."

"I love his genial and warm-hearted humour," said the old clerk.

"I have turned to the Physician's Faith," continued Riches. "I light upon the section beginning—'I never could divide myself from any man upon the difference of an opinion, or be angry with his judgment for not agreeing with me in that, from which within a few days I should dissent myself.'"

"The whole passage overflows with charity and good sense," said Peach, rubbing his hands.

"And a few leaves further on—there is a paper at the place—is the remark,— 'It is we that are blind, not fortune: because our eye is too dim to discover the mystery of her effects, we foolishly paint her blind, and hoodwink the providence of the Almighty.'"

Cornelius became rather fidgety, for he saw that the paper which Mr. Riches had mentioned lay upon the open page, and was covered with writing.

"You write yourself, my friend," observed Mr. Riches. "Will you allow me...?"

"No," answered his host, casting down his eyes. "That is, I do not write. I may sometimes jot down a thought, if a bit of paper is at hand. I cannot bear to defile the margins of my books."

"Mischievous vanity of readers," said the chaplain. "But, Mr. Peach, I like these remarks very much. Did you never print? Confess. You have caught Sir Thomas's spirit exactly." Cornelius coloured a little.

"No," said he. "Never. I have nothing to confess."

Polydore lighted his pipe, and sat down by the side of the chimney, just out of the glare of the fire. Miss Peach had retired, and the old bachelors were alone. They smoked in silence for a considerable time.

"There was a time," at length the host murmured, "when I thought I should like to print. It was when I was courting my Mabel. I fancied it would be so pleasant to present her with a volume of my own inditing. She would be proud of me. She would hear me spoken of, and would say in her heart—he belongs to me. But there was another side to the medal, something whispered me, and I had not the courage. The early ambition passed away."

"Well," said Polydore, "I was this morning singularly reminded that I had been one of the irritable race."

The old clerk's face beamed radiant among the circumambient fumes.

"You, my dear sir!" he exclaimed, and then begged pardon for the expression of surprise.

"'Tis many years ago," the chaplain said. "I had not left my university at the time. I had nearly forgotten it. Yet it was a delightful dream."

"What was your offspring?" Cornelius asked.

"A tale," was the answer. "A little story. Simple enough, but intended to promote some opinions, of which, in my youth, I was a zealous advocate. I fear I had not then learned the lesson of those first words of Sir Thomas Browne."

"I own," said Peach, "that I do not relish argumentative fiction."

"Neither, perhaps, should I now," continued Polydore. "But youth is ardent in proselytism. I dreamt over my manuscript for nights and nights. It was so true, and so interesting. I was certain it could not fail; and others thought so too. The little book would be ushered into the world in a manner more favourable than I had dared to hope. Imagine, my dear sir, the sort of intoxication with which I revised the proofs. What Gibbon calls 'the awful interval of printing' was to me a season of impatient delight. I was rushing into celebrity. And so the book appeared—by Polydore Riches. I was not yet in orders. Moreover, it was noticed by critics, on the whole, kindly. I took for granted it was selling rapidly, and prepared my emendations for a second edition. Judge then of my feelings, when, at the end of a twelvemonth, I learned that I might have spared my pains."

"What was the reason?" said Cornelius.

"I can tell you best by this," Polydore replied. "After a little idle repining, and some tacit abuse of the public mind, I laid my poor child by. I read it again in a dozen years, and I discovered a hundred defects of which I was ignorant before. No doubt the public discerned them at the first glance. I did not wonder at my disappointment."

Here again silence reigned for some time in the cosy parlour. It was broken by Mr. Peach.

"You said, my dear sir, that you were reminded of those days this morning."

"Yes," answered the chaplain. "I never could pass an open book-stall without scrutinizing the wares. It has always been one of my habits. If I were in a hurry, I should make a circuit through the side streets, instead of proceeding direct along Holborn, so irresistible is the temptation. Well, this morning I was wending my way by that great thoroughfare, and duly pausing at each successive treasure-house, when at one of them I detected an old friend. With trembling fingers, I drew the volume from between an 'Entick's Dictionary' and a 'Peregrine Pickle,' and opened it. 'By Polydore Riches.' A kind of mist came over me as I read."

"Indeed," said Mr. Peach, "it was an interesting meeting. You found yourself, as one may say, face to face with your youth."

"Exactly so. It was like shaking hands with the Riches of twenty-two. Well, the whim seized me to purchase the book, and also to ascertain the lowest value put upon it. So I went into the shop, and inquired the price. The owner ran the leaves backwards and forwards through his fingers, looked at the outside, and—but I need not trouble you with our bargaining. I bought it."

"Ah," exclaimed Cornelius, "might I beg leave to become acquainted with it?"

"You shall see the little book, if you wish, my dear sir," answered Polydore. "But listen. I do not now quite concur in the judgment of the public. I look at my offspring with parental partiality, and am fond to believe it was hardly used. And, besides, I hug the memory of my publishing days. I revel in the recollection of that one enthusiasm. And I have it all to myself. My book is forgotten. No one knows it now but myself. Would you desire to read it, my dear sir?"

Cornelius never repeated his wish. But, some time afterwards, when he had a day of leisure, he repaired to the Reading-room of the British Museum, and took down the volume of the Catalogue containing the letter R. His conscience pricked him as he did so, and if any one had then touched his elbow, or twitched his coat, he would have blushed like poor Mercy Page at Madron Well. Glancing furtively from side to side, he turned over the leaves to the page he wanted, and drew his finger down the column of names. But there was no Riches rejoicing in the Christian name of Polydore. Mr. Peach closed the tome with a feeling of relief, saying to himself,—"So, my excellent friend's book did not even find its way into this great repository. Well, I am glad I have not trespassed upon his secret."

The self-criticism in which the chaplain indulged was, perhaps, affected by the circumstances of his own history. He had strung his argument upon a story of requited but unfortunate love, and had found the tale nearly realized in his attachment to Rose Griffith. Before he was acquainted with the passion, he thought the public were right: when he had lost the mistress of his affections, he thought they were wrong. He confounded his fiction with his fact, and wove them together into a retrospective romance, the scenery of which he was reluctant to divulge.

The incident of finding his half-forgotten volume, diverted Polydore's attention from the anxieties of the moment: and we have thought the reader might not be displeased with a similar interval of repose. We must now return to the other personages of our history.

CHAPTER X.

Don Pedro. Officers, what offence have these men done?

Dogberry. Marry, sir, they have committed false report;
moreover, they have spoken untruths; secondarily, they are
slanders; sixth, and lastly, they have belied a lady; thirdly,
they have verified unjust things; and, to conclude, they are
lying knaves.

SHAKSPEARE.

The answers which the returning fugitives received to their letters during
their journey back to London, were ill calculated to restore them to serenity.
Helen acknowledged her brother's account of his marriage in a letter, which
all her affection could not prevent from betraying her grief; and Polydore
Riches, in another, did not attempt to conceal his disapproval and regret.
And he communicated to Randolph the information he had received from
Mr. Winter that proceedings were already begun to deprive him and his sister
of the little personal property which they might fancy was still their own, and
that so far the lawyer saw no hope of resisting the attempt with success. On
the other hand, Gertrude, seriously alarmed at the state of depression into
which Mrs. Pendarrel had fallen, could not help pointing out to her sister the
consequences of her imprudence. "Why did you not come to me?" she wrote;
"why did you not rely upon the support which I always promised? It might
have been only a temporary succour, but time might have done everything.
You little think, perhaps, how much distress you have occasioned by your
haste."

These letters led to a painful scene between the travellers. It was true that in
what they said self-reproach predominated, and they did not accuse each
other. But that which wears the appearance of confession, must also show
like repentance. And so when Randolph, with much bitterness, charged
himself with having brought his wife to misery, his words seemed to imply a
desire to undo what was irrevocable. And when Mildred blamed herself for
her mother's anguish, her husband might think she regretted her devotion to
him. Each tacitly acknowledged the futility of the arguments by which they
had before justified their step; and each, while pretending to accept the fault,
was jealous of the manner in which the other claimed it.

Yet they loved one another passionately and devotedly; but they found that
passion was not happiness, and that devotedness was not esteem. Tell them
they must part, and they would rush to one another, and vow it should only

be in death. Remind them how they met, and they would shrink from one another, and hang their heads in sorrow. When they thought only of themselves, their hearts beat together with a tenderness that seemed inexhaustible. When they remembered those who ought to be their friends, they turned away from each other with a sadness that chilled their blood. Now there are twenty-four hours between two risings of the sun, and even newly-married lovers cannot be looking into one another's eyes the whole of the time. Let Randolph and his bride hasten to town before they are weary of the day.

There, friends are still assiduous in their behalf. Hopeless, at present, or imprudent, it may be to try to soothe the wounded heart of a mother; better, perhaps, to wait until the first irritation has subsided. But this new piece of chicane may stimulate our zeal in unravelling what we believe to have been a foul plot. Surely some clue must be discoverable to the intricacies of this curious law-story. It is what Rereworth thinks; consoling himself for the loss of those pleasant hours when he disentangled skeins of silk. For Helen is sad, and sees no company now. Nay, Mrs. Winston thinks her residence at her house is growing a questionable point, and her husband, the philosopher, owns that it may become awkward. Yet she shall sojourn a little longer, although an apartment is vacant for her at the peachery, and Polydore Riches is there alone, and would be glad of his old pupil's society.

At length there arises a gleam of hope. Fortune may have swung the orphans' lot past the lowermost point of her wheel. Rereworth found a note on his breakfast-table at chambers one morning, containing an invitation which almost banished his appetite, although it promised no support for the body.

The rendezvous was appointed at an obscure locality in Lambeth. Seymour took a boat at the Temple-stairs, told the waterman his destination, and desired to be landed as near it as possible.

"Ask your pardon, sir," said red jacket, tossing his sculls into the rowlocks, "that's a queer place for a gentleman to want."

"Pull away, friend," answered the fare, who was not in a colloquial humour, and discouraged the talkativeness of Dogget's prizeman.

It was a delightful April morning, and the trim wherry sped steadily and swiftly over the bright water, unmolested by those floating omnibusses which of late years have increased the utility and diminished the pleasantness of London's noble river. Past the grey fortress, founded by Archbishop Baldwin, as a refuge from the indignity of personal conflicts with his monks at Canterbury, swept the boat, and drew up alongside some stairs not very far beyond. Rereworth bade the waterman await his return, and accepted the offer of "Jack" to conduct him to the place he sought.

So guided, Seymour proceeded up a narrow and unpaved lane, between high and irregular palisades; beyond which, on either hand, kilns were at work, emitting fumes far from agreeable. This passage led to a winding street, scarcely wider than itself, from which lofty windowless walls nearly excluded the light of day, and bespoke industry busy within. The dwelling-houses were mostly dingy and dismal in appearance, but at intervals might be seen one neater than usual, in whose casements a few unfortunate flowers—luxuries wherewith we have lately been surprised to learn the children of labour have no concern—lamented the absence of the sun. Rereworth's guide pointed along this uninviting thoroughfare to a sign at no great distance, and told him that was the place for which he had inquired. It was a public-house of disreputable aspect.

Seymour set his foot in the vile tavern with some repugnance, and had not replied to the question—what he would please to take—when it was answered for him by the voice of the man who had invited him to the rendezvous.

"Brandy," Everope said, and beckoned Rereworth into the parlour from which he had emerged. Seymour obeyed the signal, marvelling and sorrowing at the changed appearance of the spendthrift. It was not improved since his meeting with Michael Sinson in the park. Then he was miserable, now he was desperate. The recklessness was upon him which follows the loss of hope. With an eager but trembling hand he lifted a glass of the fire-water to his scarlet lips, and seemed to drink with the thirst of Tantalus. His visitor, shocked and distressed, could not utter a word.

"Seymour Rereworth," then said Everope, as one who had meditated on what he was going to tell; "you see a lost and desperate man. I care for nothing. Nothing cares for me. I hardly know what has prompted me to this step. But this man endeavoured once to do me a service. And I returned it by entering the service of his deadly foe. But Michael Sinson has the devil's craft as well as his malice. His net was round me before I was aware. I struggled in the meshes, but they were too strong. One by one my feelings went to sleep. I was a slave, and did my work, and earned my wages. Ay, sir, till only the other day. Till that day when I asked him for a pittance, and he struck me to the ground. That was to be my payment for the future. The blow snapped all the cords of his net. Said he, that I was worthless? No offer he could make would buy my silence now.

"You of course remember the late trial at Bodmin. You should have had me at your elbow, when you examined Michael Sinson. It was indeed he, who got up, or concocted the case for the plaintiff. I only know my own share in it. Can you imagine the temptation required to induce one who has been like me, to come and be sworn to tell the truth, with a falsehood ready framed upon his lips? You foresee what is coming. My story was learned by rote, well prepared, often rehearsed. I was armed at all points, furnished with answers to all questions. You know how I went through the ordeal.

"Yet I was nearly overthrown. I never dreamed of the defendant as being in any manner known to me. Who was Randolph Trevethlan? What did I care about the stranger? What was his ruin to me, so I won my hire? After what I have said, you will not credit the emotion, with which, in answer to the question suggested by yourself, I saw Morton rise and confront me, and remembered that he had once offered me assistance, which might have saved me from the position I then occupied.

"I quailed for a moment under his eye, but rallied immediately. I was not yet ready to avow my shame. But the memory of that moment has haunted me ever since. The idea that I had ruined him who might have averted my own fall, has rankled in my heart. I have stifled it in riot and delirium. But I had no longer the means. Sinson, my employer, reduced his scanty dole, and urged me to hide myself in a foreign land. But, no; that was not to be the reward of service such as mine. If he could extort the means of indulgence from those whom his treachery had profited, so could I from him. It was on such an errand I was bent, when he told me contemptuously I was of no use to him, and in answer to his right name, struck me to the earth. The knaves fell out, and honest men may get their own.

"You have heard my tale. I will verify it in detail in any way you please. And that done, I retire from the scene. I do not suppose you will desire to pursue me, nor do I care if you do. Would you know wherefore I am here? I dare not look respectability in the face. Even the haunts of the disreputable I have been forced to shun. Did I not there, in the midst of hollow revelry, once meet the glance of my victim? But all is over now. I am struck to the ground, and have neither the power nor the wish to rise. I want no pity, and I merit no thanks. A few shillings to keep me till my task is done, and then let me die. There's none will shed a tear."

"Mr. Everope," Rereworth said, gravely and sadly, "what you have this day done, shows that all is not lost for you. No man who lives is lost. And I, sir, trust that this is your beginning of a new existence. Are you not already in some measure comforted? Do you not feel some relief? Trust me comfort and relief will come. And do not underrate your service. It is not only Mr. Trevethlan you have benefited, but also his gentle sister, living in the apprehension of want."

"Spare me," the spendthrift cried, covering his face with his hands, "I once had sisters of my own."

"For their sake, then," Seymour said, "for the sake of everything that was ever dear to you, and may be again, arise from this unmanly despair. Will you not leave this miserable haunt? Will you not come with me?"

Everope shook his head, without raising it from his hands.

"Not now," he muttered, "not in the day-light. Wait till the darkness. Then perhaps I may seek my old abode."

"Well, well," Rereworth continued; "I will not urge you now. But this statement must be prepared for verification. You will give it me in writing."

The spendthrift assented with a nod. Paper, pen, and ink, were procured. Everope made an attempt to write, but his nerves failed him.

"Take the pen," he said; "I will dictate and sign."

Seymour complied, and took down the confession at considerable length. His wretched informant traced the whole history of his connection with Michael Sinson; the means by which he had been entrapped into the first step; the journey to Cornwall; the concoction of the evidence; his examination by Mr. Truby; his appearance at the trial. Thus, if his present tale were believed, it would entirely reverse the effect of his former testimony.

"That is all," he said, as he signed his name. "To-night I will return to my old residence. That is, if I am still free; for this Sinson holds notes of mine, on which he might cast me into the Fleet. It is what he has often threatened."

"Fear not," Rereworth answered. "I will undertake all those obligations shall be satisfied. To-morrow you must be prepared to attest your statement."

He placed a small sum of money on the table beside the spendthrift, and, having again entreated him to hope, and assured him of the means of retrieving himself, returned in a very thoughtful mood to the stairs where he had left his wherry.

Well, perhaps, it would have been, had Rereworth not parted with his penitent, until he had placed him under some surveillance. He might have been prompted to confession by transient compunction, and might want courage to persevere; or the thought of public and inevitable disgrace might drive him to despair. But Seymour was too much moved by the unhappy man's condition to oppose his desire for the shelter of night to come forth from his lair.

He made no delay at the Temple on his return, but proceeded straight to Mr. Winter's office. The worthy lawyer's eyes sparkled as he read the confession. Yet he observed it would be desirable to have it confirmed, if possible. After all, it *was* a confession, and the testimony of an accomplice is always doubtful.

There might be some question which story should be believed, the first or the second. On the face of the statement there appeared personal reasons for making it. The deponent might be influenced by rancour against his late employer.

"Oh, never mind, my good sir," cried Rereworth; "have that statement put into a shape for attestation, and, trust me, it will be maintained."

"Ay, ay," answered Winter; "and it will be a pleasant wedding present to meet our friend on his return."

The suggestion was scarcely agreeable to Rereworth. He went back to his chambers, and read carefully through his notes of the trial at Bodmin; and he wrote Mr. Riches a short account of his discovery.

CHAPTER XI.

And this the world calls frenzy. But the wise
Have a far deeper madness, and the glance
Of melancholy is a fearful gift.
What is it but the telescope of truth?
Which strips the distance of its fantasies,
And brings life near in utter nakedness,
Making the cold reality too real.

BYRON.

It is a misfortune for the historian that he is unable to present events as they really happened, simultaneously, but must be content to relate them one after another, thereby unavoidably impressing his reader with a false idea of the lapse of time. The same morning that Rereworth made his expedition to Lambeth, Mrs. Pendarrel paid a visit to her daughter in Cavendish Square. Restless, but languid; dejected, but unforgiving, she came to vent her querulousness on Mrs. Winston, in complaint and reproach. She wished also to learn, without showing the desire, what news had reached town respecting the fugitives. She could not close her heart entirely against the memory of her child. She liked to hear her mentioned, even when she answered the intelligence with anger and contempt. And so she came to Gertrude almost daily, to listen and to abuse.

She now entered the house, as usual, without ceremony, and proceeded to the room where she commonly found Mrs. Winston; but on this occasion Gertrude was not there. Her mother looked listlessly at two or three of the books upon the table, and wandered into the adjoining apartment, absent in mind, but disappointed at not seeing her she sought. Here she lingered a few minutes more, and then passed on into the smaller room, where, as she well recollected, she had encountered Randolph Trevethlan. A young lady, sitting with her back to the door, turned as it opened, and Mrs. Pendarrel immediately recognized Randolph's companion at the opera, his sister. Helen also remembered the original of her miniature, and rose from her chair as Esther advanced.

"What!" the last-named lady exclaimed, fixing her keen eyes upon Helen. "Have I been mocked? Have I been the sport of a paltry conspiracy? Has my daughter been nursing the thief, and condoling with me upon the robbery? Fawning upon me with hypocritical lamentations, and sheltering those who wronged me? For I see it all. It was here the plot was hatched; here the correspondence was managed; here the flight was arranged. Did not

Gertrude always boast that she would thwart my schemes? Yet I hardly thought she would go so far as this."

"Madam," Helen ejaculated in great confusion, "madam, you do Mrs. Winston wrong. She knew nothing of my brother's design. Neither did I. But let your blame only fall on me, for I was the unconscious means of its execution."

"Do you dare to answer me, Miss Trevethlan?" Esther asked angrily. "And what do you here? What does one of your name in the house of one of mine? Name! What is your name? You have none. What business has one like you to be here?"

"I am an intruder, madam," Helen answered, the tears rising in her soft eyes—"I have felt it, and know it. But I came here before this unhappy matter. The invitation was very kind. We were very poor. I would relieve my brother."

"Poor! did you say, Miss Trevethlan?" exclaimed Esther. "Yes; and you will be still poorer before many days are gone! Unhappy? No, no; you did not think so. The beggar does not call it unhappy when he inveigles away a rich heiress. But it is a mistake. She has nothing. You will be no richer for the stolen marriage; neither you nor your brother, Miss Trevethlan."

"Oh, madam," said Helen in much distress, "I wish you could read in my heart. You would spare me these reproaches. You do not know how I deplore what has occurred. The loss of our home, the poverty and sorrow you speak of, everything I would have endured, rather than my brother had done this. We want nothing of you, madam, nothing but forgiveness; and you may spare sarcasms which are undeserved."

"Would your brother ask my forgiveness?" said Mrs. Pendarrel. "Was there a word of the kind in Mildred's letter? No, Miss Trevethlan; forgiveness will never be asked, and never be granted. Why; do you not hate me yourself? You must have learned from infancy to detest my name. Was not Pendarrel pointed at as the destroyer of Trevethlan? Am not I the author of the desolation which has fallen upon your head? Truly, Miss Trevethlan, it might rouse your father's spirit from his grave, to feel that one of his children dwelt under the roof of one of mine."

"No, madam," Helen exclaimed, almost as vehemently as she was addressed—"a thousand times no. Not till lately did I know there was any difference."

"'Tis untrue!" said Esther. "'Tis nonsense. You were born to hate. You were bequeathed an inheritance of hate. You accepted it. Did not you send me with scorn from your doors? It was your turn then. It is mine now. Hate breeds hate."

"And on which side did it begin, if it were so?" Helen asked. "On ours? Madam, were we not treated as if hatred were indeed our only inheritance? Was not my brother insulted with an offer of charity? I speak his mind, and not my own, for I thought the offer was kind. But I see now that he was right."

"You will be glad to have the offer repeated ere long," said Esther bitterly.

"You wronged us then, madam," Helen said, "and you wrong us now. We, alone on the earth, young, mourning the only parent we had ever known, little likely were we to hate our nearest connections. Was hatred bequeathed to us? No, madam. I might deem our inherited feelings were far other, for this portrait was the last companion of our poor father. They found it upon his heart when he died."

Esther caught the miniature from Helen's hand, and gazed earnestly at it for some seconds. Then she pressed it to her lips in a kind of ecstacy.

"He loved me to the last," she murmured.

But the transport passed away as rapidly as it came. Melancholy, stern and dark, fell over Mrs. Pendarrel's brow. She clasped the miniature upon her bosom.

"Girl," she said, almost in a whisper, "you give me great joy and sorrow inexpressible. I have been desperately wronged. My life has been a blank. I cannot change on a sudden. I do not know what to think. Let me keep this portrait."

And she departed from the room and from the house, leaving Helen bewildered by a host of perplexing reflections. She remembered what Randolph said concerning that miniature, but she was unaware of the promise exacted from him at their father's death-bed. She scarcely understood in what manner the law-suit had been only the final step in a career of vengeance. But she felt that she had been grievously insulted, and she perceived the ambiguity of her situation at Mrs. Winston's. She resolved on returning to Hampstead without delay.

It was a pity, for she had been an angel of peace to Gertrude. She had taught the husband and wife to know one another, and the knowledge might soon become affection. Yet her hostess confessed to herself that the resolution was correct, even though she was ignorant of the conversation which had immediately inspired it. She did not so much as attempt to delay its execution, and the same afternoon found Helen once more an inmate of Mr. Peach's modest, but pleasant and pretty dwelling.

Comfort followed her there. Rereworth's letter to Polydore Riches came to revive hope, and to bring oblivion of the affronts and menaces of the morning. The news exhilarated the chaplain's drooping spirits, and inclined him to regard the elopement with less severity. And Helen thought with gratitude of the writer, and perhaps remembered those readings of Scott and Byron in Mrs. Winston's little drawing-room.

Besides this, the fugitives were now approaching the metropolis, and might possibly arrive the same night. Here were copious sources of conversation to fill the evening when the chaplain talked with Helen in the pleasant parlour, where she had sat during the past winter, and which had witnessed the extinction of all those hopes, so long and so fondly cherished at Trevethlan Castle, the day-dreams of Merlin's Cave.

If Mrs. Pendarrel inflicted much pain in her short interview with Helen, she did not quit it herself unscathed. The sight of her portrait aroused a thousand recollections, familiar indeed to Esther's hours of reverie, but never so vividly presented before. She thought of the day when she permitted that miniature to be taken from her neck. In the morning she hung it there, not without an idea that it might pass into another's possession before night. Often had the favour been solicited by the lover, and as often refused by the coquette. But at last assiduity might triumph over waywardness. Side by side they strolled over the lawns of Pendarrel, enjoying converse such as is only derided by the unhappy wights who have never shared it. There was a secluded little pool, formed by the rivulet which murmured through the wilderness, surrounded by flowering shrubs, and over-arched so closely by spreading forest-trees, that the sunshine scarcely penetrated to the surface of the water. It was in that bower, under the thickest of the leafy canopy, that Henry Trevethlan detached the miniature from the chain by which it hung, and his lips met those of Esther in the first kiss of love. How well she remembered it now! Every little circumstance, the attitude in which they stood, the few whispered words, came back to her mind, fresh as the things of yesterday. A bright-winged butterfly alighted for a moment upon her wrist, and he called her Psyche, his soul, without whom he should die. The butterfly rested but a second—was its flight ominous of what had occurred since? And had he virtually died? Had his subsequent existence been a mere life in death? Had his soul indeed remained always with her? So, Esther thought, it would seem. And had he forgiven the ruin into which he was driven by despair? Had he pardoned the despair itself, the wreck of all his hopes and feelings, the anguish which abided with him to the last?

Questions like these passed rapidly through Esther's mind, while she gazed on the fair young face which once had been her own. Very different was her aspect now. The round and glowing cheeks had become hollow and pale. The smooth white forehead was furrowed with the lines of sorrow. Silver threads mingled with the dark tresses. The eyes, in the miniature deep and inscrutable, were now wild and bright. The passions of the girl had been developed in the woman, and had left their trace on every feature.

And then Esther turned to self-justification. Had she made no atonement? Had she suffered nothing? Had her heart been unwasted? Resolutely as she had striven to repress all memory of that early dream, had she succeeded in the attempt? Was not the lava still hot beneath the foliage which grew over it? Had not the smouldering fire broken forth anew on the news of Henry's death? And again she thought she had been hardly used by the precipitation with which he abandoned her. It was cruel to afford her no chance of reconciliation. If he might charge her with vanity or wilfulness, surely she might accuse him of rancour and pride. If the happiness of her lover had been shattered by the storm, neither had her own escaped its ravages.

She had endeavoured to forget them in the gratification of her love of rule, and her eager pursuit of revenge. The first she enjoyed in the management of her own household, the second in the downfall of Trevethlan. Ambition and appetite grew with what they fed on. "Pendar'l and Trevethlan shall own one name." Not till that prediction had been fulfilled to the letter, and to her own glory, could Esther rest. Her old lover had departed from the scene; she prolonged the contest with his children. They increased her ardour by the mode in which they met her first advances. For a season she seemed to be foiled. But the check gave new vigour to her never-dying wrath.

And before long the orphans crossed her path. And soon he, the heir of all his father's pride, encountered her, face to face, as the companion of her child. She had trembled to think of what that meeting might call forth. But then she learned the tale, which would fulfil all her desires to an extent beyond her dreams, and forgot her danger in the exultation of approaching triumph. Triumph came, but only as the precursor of defeat; for her enemy, ruined and dishonoured, had suborned the affection of her daughter, and made her house desolate in the very hour of victory.

Yes, scandal made merry with the name of Pendarrel. Esther, with all her rigid discipline, with all her cherished authority, had seen the child, for whose marriage with another her word was pledged, elude her control, and steal to a furtive union with the man whom she had been labouring to bring to want and shame. It was nearly enough to deprive her of her reason. No time was this to think of forgiveness. She would not believe that Helen Trevethlan was so innocent as she pretended. The production of the miniature was a theatrical trick. The picture should revive the memory of a never-forgiven wrong.

Let the suit then be pressed. Let there be no respite. Let calamity fall fast and heavy. Let disobedience and presumption meet their just reward. But where was the agent? Where was he who had pointed out the path of revenge? What had he said when she last saw him? Better, Esther thought scornfully, better even that match than this. And what meant his dark insinuations? Had he not dared to threaten?

Langour crept over the muser. She began to grow aweary of the sun. She felt as if her self-control were slipping from her grasp. Shadowy fears beset her. She did not like to be alone. She was glad when her husband came home from his official duties; and he became seriously alarmed at her altered demeanour. She seemed to be sinking into a state of lethargy, which might affect her mind. Mr. Pendarrel sent to beg Mrs. Winston to come and watch by her mother, who was evidently very ill. And Gertrude came, but for some time her presence seemed only to irritate the invalid. It might be observed that from about this day Esther entirely discontinued her old practice of calling her husband by the name which he had abandoned to obtain her hand.

CHAPTER XII.

Anne magis Siculi gemuerunt æra juvenci,
Aut magis auratis pendens laquearibus ensis
Purpureas subter cervices terruit, *Imus*;
Imus præcipites, quam si sibi dicat, intus
Palleat infelix, quod proxima nesciat uxor?

PERSIUS.

Down, headlong, down—Say could that bull of fire,
Or thread-suspended sword such fear inspire,
As his, whose thoughts, to bosom-wife unknown,
Ring in his livid heart—*Down, headlong, down*?

That same evening the fugitive couple arrived in the metropolis, and took up their abode in apartments engaged for them by Mr. Riches at a hotel. It was time. Already they were beginning to long for other company than their own; a few days more might make their own companionship intolerable. One quarter of the moon had nearly taught them the vanity of the lover's chimera, that they were all-sufficient for one another. There was so much anxiety about their path, so much gloom around the present, so much dismay in the future, that their spirits drooped, and even love seemed to grow cold in their hearts. Let them beware, for they were united for ever. In the preservation of their mutual regard lay their only chance of peace; should that vanish, there was nothing but misery before them. The day might then come when Mildred would be qualified to receive succour from her mother, on the terms which Esther, in the fierceness of her first indignation, had not scrupled to prescribe.

The sense of the fault they had committed lay at the bottom of their discontent. Mildred repented with bitter sorrow her rupture of all filial ties, and exaggerated her sister's account of the distress it had occasioned, thinking sometimes that she might even have broken her mother's heart. She forgot the severity with which she had lately been treated, and remembered only the tenderness which she had not seldom experienced. She often recollected how she had been pressed to her mother's bosom on the night of the fire, and she trembled to dwell upon the affection which one moment had cast away.

Randolph read some portion of her thoughts; and he perceived that the maternal sorrow to which he had once looked forward with perverse eagerness, afforded him none of the satisfaction he had expected. It was not so he ought to avenge his own or his father's wrongs. The scheme recoiled upon himself. There was no happiness for him while his bride was unhappy, and nothing but wretchednes for her until she had made her peace at home. And so Randolph saw that his stolen marriage had actually contributed to Esther's triumph. She had now not only his worldly wealth, but himself beneath her foot. He had placed himself in a position where he must either sue for mercy or behold his wife pining away before his eyes.

Amidst such gloomy speculations, one bright spot sometimes appeared to his mental vision. "I have thought," his father said, in those well remembered words, "she was not so indifferent to me as she chose to pretend. If it were so, she has avenged me on herself, and has my forgiveness." Would that Randolph had dwelt oftener upon the hope contained in this qualification, and more seldom upon the stern injunction! Would that he had not suffered the early affront to himself to take so firm a hold of him! That he had not fomented his personal quarrel, until now he could see no avenue to reconciliation! That he had listened with more humility to the remonstrances of Polydore Riches!

These wishes were idle now. It was a sad evening of the honeymoon when Randolph and his bride sat together in their hired and temporary abode, having none of their own, and hardly daring to consider what would become of them. In slow and broken sentences they discussed their future prospects, and strove to cheer one another with hopes in which neither put any trust.

At an early hour in the morning, Randolph escorted Mildred to her sister's, and left her there, he himself proceeding to Hampstead. Gertrude had no consolation to offer the young wife. Indeed, she was obliged to own that Mrs. Pendarrel was in a condition to cause considerable alarm. She said it would be dangerous for Mildred to present herself, and would only permit her to call in the carriage at the house in May Fair and remain at the door, while she herself ascertained their mother's state. It was not satisfactory; and Gertrude resumed her watch; while Mildred returned in increased solicitude to such distraction as could be supplied by her attendant. Sorely puzzled was Rhoda at so woeful a termination to an elopement.

Meantime, Randolph continued on his way to the dwelling which had sheltered himself and Helen in the first enthusiasm of their arrival in the metropolis. Little had they then deemed how soon that enthusiasm was to be chilled; little they thought how soon they would return to their home by the sea with all their hopes extinguished. And still less could they know, that even that brief absence would be pregnant with events to influence their whole lives; and that whereas when they quitted their birth-place they were heart-whole and fancy-free, one of them, at least, would return to it the slave of passion and unable to hope.

They had lost that home since then. They had bidden farewell, and, as they might at times fear, for ever, to the scenes endeared by a thousand recollections. Thenceforth they could only lean upon one another. And suddenly they were separated. The brother, rashly and wrongfully, had taken another partner in misfortune, and abandoned the former sharer of his affections. And now, with such feelings, they once more met. Yet, amidst all these mournful reminiscences, Randolph felt some relief from his trouble in Helen's greeting. She inquired very warmly for her sister, and he was delighted at hearing the word.

She told him of her interview with Mrs. Pendarrel the morning before, and he listened with a degree of interest which surprised her. He questioned her eagerly respecting every word that was uttered, and his cheeks flushed with anger when he extorted from the narrator an account of Mrs. Pendarrel's insults. But this expression seemed to pass away, when Helen described the emotion displayed by Esther at the sight of her own likeness, and the whispered exclamation—"He loved me to the last!"

"There is hope for us, Helen," the brother said, "in your words. If I am right in interpreting them, there is hope I may find peace for my Mildred. I have a key to them which you know not of. But, alas! we must first re-establish ourselves."

"And of that, too, there is hope," said Helen. "Go to Mr. Riches: let him have the pleasure of telling you the news. It only came last night. From your friend,—but our dear chaplain will tell you all the story."

So to Polydore, Randolph went, and learned the discovery which Rereworth had made. It certainly gave him great joy, although it was communicated very gravely. The chaplain did not affect to conceal his mortification at his old pupil's dereliction of the right path. He urged the necessity of sacrificing every personal feeling in order to procure a reconciliation with Mildred's family.

"It is not so very long," he said, "since you spoke to me of an inherited quarrel and injunctions of revenge. Such thoughts must be laid aside now. They were before uncharitable and wrong, but now they are actively pernicious. I shall have no comfort till I know that peace has been made."

Randolph subdued some rising impatience, and answered that he had conceived some hopes of so desirable a result.

"And, my dear sir," he continued, "we desire, Mildred and I, that you would hallow our union. As soon as possible we shall be re-married, and we hope for your blessing."

"Then the bride's parents must be present to sanction it," Polydore answered. "With that condition, nothing could afford me so great a pleasure."

Randolph sighed, and departed on his return to town. But his heart was much lighter than when he went. He had also much to do, and the necessary activity diverted his melancholy. First, he must call upon Rereworth, and learn the details of this confession of Everope's, which afforded hope of recovering his rights, and restoring his father's honour. For this purpose he bent his way straight to the Temple.

Seymour met him with congratulatory rebukes, uttered between jest and earnest, and declared that he would never have presented Mr. Morton at Mr. Winston's, had he been at all aware of his wicked ways. He also indulged in some facetiousness respecting the defendant's running off with the plaintiff's daughter, and remarked that a wife was scarcely a desirable commodity where there was no property at all either to give or receive. His tone showed his confidence in the approach of a happy dénouement. Randolph forced a smile, and turned the conversation to the story of Everope.

"Ah," Seymour said, becoming grave in his turn, "that's a bad business. He was to have sworn to his tale this morning, and when I went to see after him, he was no more. He died by his own hand. In the night. I have reproached myself ever since I parted from him yesterday, for allowing him to be alone. And now his death puts us in a little difficulty. I must become a witness. But there. You can read the narrative, as I took it down from his lips. And then we will go and talk over the affair at Winter's. I understand Everope's accomplice is now down in the country."

Randolph read the confession with eager eyes. He saw that Everope's remorse had perhaps originated in his recognition of himself at the trial, as having once offered to do him some trifling service. He wished he had arrived in time to repeat the offer, and possibly to save the spendthrift from destruction. When he had finished the perusal, he and Rereworth set forth on their way to Mr. Winter's offices.

They had to pass the foot of Everope's staircase. A group of persons, laundresses and porters, such as may often be seen gossiping in the inns of court, was congregated at the entrance, conversing earnestly, but in low tones. Rereworth made his companion acquainted with the few details he had been able to collect, or to conjecture, concerning the unhappy suicide.

He had gone to Everope's rooms in good time, to prepare him to attest his confession, and had even then been detained by a crowd like that which was still there. He made his way without much heed, being in fact preoccupied, and rapped at the spendthrift's door. The old laundress answered the knock, seemed greatly surprised when he inquired for her master, and raised the corner of her apron to her eyes.

"What is the matter, ma'am?" Rereworth asked. "What has happened?" And he remembered the groups below with some alarm.

A few broken words made him acquainted with the catastrophe.

Everope, it seemed, had come home late in the night. He had obtained a light, and had been engaged in looking over a quantity of correspondence and other papers, for such were found strewn about the floor of his room. Letters of old date, some written when he must have been quite a youth, lay open on the table. Were the recollections they aroused more than his shattered, perhaps delirious, senses could bear? Such Rereworth fancied must have been the case.

He had glanced slightly at some of the scattered papers, and then recoiled from prying into matters which concerned him not. One scrap, however, freshly written upon, caught his eye, and he found it to contain a few stanzas of verse, evidently penned long ago, and some incoherent attempts to continue them, which must have been made that very night. He took possession of this document, in order to produce it, if necessary; and he now showed it to his friend. And Randolph, in reading the following melancholy lines, the older portion of the writing, thought with shuddering pity of the whisper, once addressed by Everope to himself, which had called forth his offer of assistance.

'Tis sad to think of hopes destroyed,
Of prospects lost that once seemed fair,
Of hours in waste or vice employed,
Of talents as *that* fig-tree bare.

Where ruin watches the closed door,
And crouches on the cold hearth-stone,
Where home's a word of love no more,
And friends or kindred there are none;

What though the door exclude the wind?
What though the roof may shield from rain?
No winds like those that tear the mind,
No storms like those that rend the brain.

While stern remorse unfolds her scroll,
And points to every damning word,

Showing the late-repenting soul
All it has thought, done, seen, or heard—

Ay, press thy hands upon thine eyes,
Ay, hear not, feel not, if thou wilt!
Still memory to conscience cries,
Still every heart-quake throbs of guilt.

Think over all thou might'st have been,
Contrast it then with all thou art:
A retrospect so dark and keen
May well appal thy shuddering heart.

Woe for the days when childhood knelt
At night and morn its prayer to say;
Breathed worship such as childhood felt,
And loved the vows it learned to pay!

But now—but now—can phrenzy pray?
To Heaven shall desperation cry?
Madness prepares destruction's way—
Escape is none—despair, and die!

"That," said Rereworth, when Randolph gave him back the paper, "is the superficial penitence, which never does any good. It is regret for the effects of the fault, not for the fault itself. In true repentance there is always hope, but in such feelings as are here portrayed there is little else than despair. Hence this miserable end."

"Yet," Randolph urged, with some discontent at the moralizing of his friend, "he seems to have been meant for better things."

"Few men are not," answered Rereworth. "Few men are not meant for better things than they achieve. Short-coming is the rule, and fulfilling the exception. But a truce with what sounds misanthropical. Here we are at Winter's."

The lawyer heard of the suicide with much commiseration.

"But," said he, "our feelings must not interfere with business. This confession, verified by you, Mr. Rereworth, ought to carry us to the bottom of the matter. I wish we could get at the true circumstances of the marriage. You see the real insinuation is, that the late Mr. Trevethlan was privy to the death of Ashton, and the spiriting away of the witness. I wish, with all my heart, we could clear up the mystery."

And Randolph felt that there could be no rest for him until the entire groundlessness of so dark an impeachment was made clear to all the world.

CHAPTER XIII.

From house to house, from street to street,
The rapid rumour flies;
Incredulous ears it finds, and hands
Are lifted in surprise;
And tongues through all the astonished town
Are busier now than eyes.

SOUTHEY.

"So, Mistress Miniver, the old house is like to wear a new sign before many days. There'll be a change in the arms, methinks."

"Not while my name's Miniver, Master Colan," answered the plump hostess of the Trevethlan Arms.

"Maybe you'd not object to change that, dame," suggested the farmer.

Mrs. Miniver played with a well-sized bunch of keys that hung from her girdle.

"Ay, ay," said Colan—

"'The key of the locker the good-wife keeps, The good-wife's busy, the good-man sleeps.'

"I fancy you sat in St. Michael's chair the day you were married, Mistress Miniver."

"I'll tell you one who did, farmer," said the hostess, laughing merrily; "and that's the lady of Pendar'l. God forbid I should ever say of Trevethlan! And d'ye mind what I said, Master Colan? Didn't I foretell what would happen if ever Squire Randolph and Miss Mildred came together? And you see they're wooed and married and all."

"There's not much good like to come of it for Trevethlan," observed the farmer. "They say the mother's as cold as stone."

"Mayhap some folks wouldn't care if she were," said Germoe the tailor, who had come up during the last few words.

"Oh, neighbours," cried the light-hearted hostess, thrusting her hands into the pockets of her white apron, "take my word, it'll all come right in the end. It's natural to fret and fume a little, but it all blows over. The squire'll bring home his bride by furry-time, I warrant."

"'Twill be time he did," quoth Germoe; "for the castle's getting awful lonesome and dismal. How Mr. Griffith and his dame can bide there, is more than I can tell; and, as for old Jeffrey, he's as dumb as any of the ghosts they say walk there."

"Tales to quiet babes, friend Germoe," said Mrs. Miniver. "Old Jeffrey'll run up our flag again before the oak's in leaf."

"You were always so comfortable, dame," remarked Colan. "But how'll they get over the trial at Bodmin yonder? There's an uncommon mystery about that marriage, Mistress Miniver."

"Tell you what, farmer," quoth the hostess more gravely, "I care a deal more for our poor folks that are in the jail at Bodmin. Do you know, they say it's a hanging matter?"

"And our Mercy's sweetheart among them, dame," said Germoe.

"If our Mercy's sweetheart is there," Mrs. Miniver said, "it is to bring them to ruin. And I heard he did come down here a little ago. It's young Sinson, I mean, Master Germoe."

"They say his old grandame takes on quite fearful-like," said Breage the general merchant, who now joined the little party under the shade of the old chestnut. "She sits all day, moaning, and rocking herself, and breaks out with something about her daughter, our late squire's lady, and then brings herself up quite short."

"Her Michael's plenty on his mind, neighbours," quoth Mrs. Miniver; "you may take your oath of that. I don't wonder old Maud's a bit uneasy. But, hey-day! who comes here?"

For a horseman rode rapidly on to the far end of the green, crossed it straight without drawing rein, and proceeded up the ascent of the base-court.

"What's in the wind now?" asked farmer Colan.

But curiosity tied the tongues of the circle. They watched the stranger while he held a short parley with Jeffrey, and at last dismounted with apparent impatience, and attached his bridle to a ring in the wall. The old porter opened the gate and conducted him within, soon emerging again himself, and seeming to examine the panting quadruped at the porch.

Several of the villagers came and joined the group beneath the chestnut. They soon began to discuss this visit in low voices. Whether fear or hope predominated in their explanations, it might not be easy to determine. But the freshness of a sunny April morning might seem likely to inspire the latter feeling, even as it had been evident in Mrs. Miniver's share of the dialogue recorded above.

Presently Griffith was seen to come forth from the castle-gate, and after exchanging a few words with Jeffrey, to descend the hill with the stranger, who took his reins upon his arm. The excitement of the villagers increased. As the steward drew near, a similar expression might be read in his own face. He came up and told Mrs. Miniver he wanted the one chaise which she still kept, got ready immediately. A dozen voices demanded the news.

"I hardly know what to say, my friends," Griffith answered. "But if the tidings are well founded, they are good news for all who love Trevethlan."

"Hurrah," shouted the assembly.

It was a work of some little time to prepare Mrs. Miniver's chaise, for the horses which were to draw it, were usually engaged in agricultural pursuits. But it was ready at last, and the steward drove off.

The stranger remained to give his animal rest, and was of course assailed with a host of questions. But all he could say was that an attorney at Bodmin had sent him with a letter to Mr. Griffith of Trevethlan Castle, and especially desired him to lose no time on the road. In about an hour he remounted, and rode away in a more leisurely manner than he had arrived.

In order to explain the occurrence which caused so much commotion in the hamlet, we must revert to the proceedings of Michael Sinson. Smarting under the discomfiture of all his long-cherished desires, driven ignominiously from the house of his patroness, and attributing his fall to the man against whom he had borne hatred even from childhood, Michael left London, with the intention of trying to implicate Randolph in the burning of Pendarrel. He imagined that he had a perfect hold upon his mistress in spite of her proud indifference, and turned his immediate attention to the overthrow of his successful rival. Restless and cunning, he was never happy now except when engaged in some intrigue, and his recent triumph at Bodmin had given him new zest for the work.

With such ideas he obtained admission to the prisoners charged with the incendiarism, and sought, as craftily as he could, to extract some information reflecting upon the disinherited owner of Trevethlan Castle. But he sought in vain: there were no tidings of the kind to give. Then Sinson went to his old grandmother, and bore her peevish humours for a short time, still seeking intelligence to further his designs. He met his too faithful Mercy, and endeavoured to find such in her knowledge of what passed within the castle walls. But again he was baffled. He had to deal with natures very different from his own.

Finally, he once more repaired to the congenial atmosphere of the gaol, and tried to gain the confidence of the ringleader of the mob, Gabriel Denis. Here he met his match. The old smuggler was as wary as himself. He bent an attentive ear to Michael's suggestions, how it was supposed the fire was the result of a long-devised plot, how a considerable reward would be paid, and a free pardon granted to any one who would furnish a true history of the affair. And Sinson insinuated dark hints concerning the late owner of Trevethlan, how he had a quarrel of many years' standing with the family of Pendarrel, how some people thought he was in the secret of the incendiaries, and how, if it were so, his impeachment would be the means of liberating a number of the inferior criminals. In short, Gabriel drew him on, until by degrees he had disclosed all his plan, and the smuggler was fully aware, that, true or false, a certain story would bring a certain price.

Now in prison, Denis had become rather intimate with Edward Owen. They both kept somewhat apart from their accused confederates. And Gabriel was full of wild adventure, in different quarters of the globe, which served to while away the dreary hours of confinement. So, among other things, the smuggler told Owen of the suggestions which were made to him by Sinson. The young peasant started.

"That's the villain that betrayed my master in the trial the other day," he said. "Have nought to say to him, Gabriel. He'd sell his best friend. I ought to know him well. He's driven the squire from the castle, and now he would bring him to shame. No, no; the squire knew nought about the fire, that I can warrant."

"Trust me, Edward," Denis answered; "I am too deep for him by a fathom and a half. But what's this ye say about the squire? Driven from the castle?"

"Did ye not hear then," said Owen. "This Michael brought a fellow to swear away the marriage of the last squire, and so they are going to turn the son out of the castle. It passes to them whose house was burned. And Michael is in their pay. Sorrow on the day when a Trevethlan took a bride from under the thatch."

"I ought to mind that day well," the smuggler said, musing.

"You!" Owen exclaimed.

"'T will be twenty-one-two-three, twenty-three years, next September. I mind it well. The parson was killed. What did folks say about it?"

"I was scarce born," Edward answered. "But I ha' heard it made a great noise in the country. Some said it was Will Watch's people, and some that the Squire knew more about it than he'd choose to tell."

"That was wrong," said Denis.

"What!" cried his companion.

"I mean 'twas none of his people at the time. And what's this ye say about the marriage?"

"Well, it was always thought to be made by this parson, whose body they found under the cliff. But now Michael brings a fellow to swear 'twas no such thing, but he married them himself, and, he not being a parson, the marriage falls to the ground, and the squire's son is put out of the castle. That's what it is."

The smuggler mused for some time.

"Edward," then he said, "'tis a long time since that night, and little I deemed to have it brought back like this. I have sailed many a league since then, and half of it has been forgotten. And why should I recollect it to-day? Will it do me good or harm? But there's nought left me to care for now; nought but the little lass that the revenue thieves carried off when they had shot my poor Felipa. And then this fire; one can hardly be worse off than one is. And I should like to put a check on this sneaking knave, that wanted to draw me into a lie. So sit thee down, lad, and listen to the rights of all this story:—

"'Tis twenty-three years ago, I was much such another as ye are now. But, to say the truth, fonder of the wrestling-ring than of the plough, and better pleased at a wake than at a sermon. Moreover, I knew the country well, and when I set a snare at night you may rely it was not empty in the morning. Well, it was that spring or summer, there came to lodge at Madam Sennor's— a little house on the cliff, not over far from Trevethlan Castle—one Mr. Ashton, that was a clergyman. Somehow or other he fell in with me, and used to get me to guide him, as it were, about the country,—a thing that suited my idle ways very well. Now I soon found that Mr. Ashton was not over much like a parson, but did not care to go to a wake himself, and could read the glance of a girl's eye as well as another. So he and I grew to be in a way more companionable than suited my station perhaps; but I don't know it, for he was often very ill off for money. Be it as it will, we got on very well together.

"So, while we were on this footing, says Mr. Ashton to me one day,—Wyley, he says, here's Mr. Trevethlan, of the Castle, wants me to marry him specially, or something, he called it, and I am to take a witness with me. Will you come? says he. And he told me the particulars; as how it was a young peasant girl, and there would be money to be had for the business, and so I agreed to go. Well, he took me with him to the castle, and Mr. Trevethlan met us himself on the outside, and brought us just into the great hall without our seeing a single soul. And there were a young woman, and also an old one, that I understood was her mother. So Mr. Trevethlan gave Mr. Ashton a prayer-book, and he read the office between the parties, and I was put to give the bride—Margaret something was her name—away. And I recollect that

Ashton, being somewhat nervous, dropped the ring, and the mother muttered it was no good sign.

"When it was over, Mr. Trevethlan put a purse into Ashton's hand, and we went our way. But I thought there must be something wrong in the business, and therefore I chose to consider that Ashton did not give me my fair share of the price. However, it was not a thing to talk over in the high road, and I knew well where to find him. He used to walk along the cliff every evening; and there, just as it was getting dusk, I went to meet him. We had some high words, and as I came towards him he stepped backwards, not recollecting how near he was to the edge, and he went over.

"I was terribly frightened,—nothing, I knew, could go over there and live. I thought I was charged with the murder. I lay down, trembling, and put my head beyond the edge. I fancied I could see him just move. I lurked thereabout, on and off, not knowing what to do, till it came to be quite dark. Then I saw lights at one or two points, and began to think the people were already on the search. But it was not so; and the truth was all in my favour.

"The lights were the country folk's signals to Will Watch's lugger, that was then running in. Luckily for me, as I thought, she took up a berth a good way off the spot where Ashton lay. All the country turned out to run the cargo. And I crept down by myself to the beach, and came to where he had fallen, and there I found him stone-dead. I don't know what it was moved me, but I fancied that if the body were not owned nothing could be done. And, in that thought, I took off the clothes, and buried them in a nook of the cliff, which I could show to this day. For himself, I could see, by the light from the water, he was so much hurt that no one would know him. I should say, that I got the money which had been the cause of our difference. Well, when this was all over, my fears grew worse and worse. I thought it would have been better to have left him alone. At last I went among the throng of folks that were busy running the kegs, and got on board the lugger. She took me over to Holland, and from there I shipped myself for the Spanish Indies, and lived a roving life.

"But I tired of it at length, and had got a wife—my poor Felipa—and a little girl. So I came home. Lived quiet a while, until I was sure that no one knew me by my old name, and that the tale of Ashton's death was nigh forgotten, and then took to the cabin on the hill. The rest you know."

Owen listened to this narrative with wonder and joy, for he saw it would be likely to restore his squire, as he called him, to all his rights.

"But why," said he after a silence, "why then did you not come forward to claim the reward they offered?"

"I did not know of any such," Gabriel answered. "If I had, I should not have heeded it till they drove me from my cottage. It matters not now. Do what you will with the tale."

The young peasant gazed on the swarthy features which had been bronzed by near a score of year's exposure to a tropical sun, and did not marvel that the sea-faring wanderer had escaped unrecognised. He was in communication with an attorney of the town for the purposes of his own defence, and to him, with Gabriel's permission, he told the strange tale. Its importance was at once perceived and acknowledged. And the lawyer in question immediately despatched the news to Griffith by the messenger whose arrival had excited the curiosity described in the opening of this chapter. Thus Michael Sinson's artifices again recoiled upon himself; by his attempted perversion of Gabriel Denis, he cut the ground from under his own feet. He acquired some inkling of what had transpired, and hurried back to London; more vexed than before at his quarrel with Everope, of whose melancholy end he had as yet received no information.

Denis, or Wyley, was nothing loth to repeat his story. Griffith, having the knowledge which Owen was too young to possess, was able to confirm him on several points. The narrative was verified in every possible manner, and a copy transmitted to Winter, while the steward returned to Trevethlan, to confirm it still further, by disinterring the buried clothes.

In the flush of his exultation, he did not attempt to conceal the purpose of his journey, and the greater part of the villagers turned out spontaneously to assist in the quest which he undertook without loss of time. Gabriel had described with great exactitude the spot to be searched, for he remembered it very well. And indeed there were many people still living who could point out the place where the body was found. Near at hand, a long narrow rift ran into the face of the precipice, and at its extreme end, where the billows of every winter increased the depth of superincumbent sand, Wyley stated he had deposited the garments which would identify the wearer. The cleft was too narrow for more than one man to dig at a time, and the excitement of the crowd behind him increased with every stroke of his spade. The smuggler appeared to have told the truth. A quantity of half-destroyed garments were discovered, and among them a pocket-book containing a pencil-case and a ring. The clothes were worthless for any object; but of these last-mentioned articles Griffith took possession, and forwarded them to London, in order that they might be submitted to Mr. Ashton's friends for recognition.

"Hurrah for Trevethlan!" shouted Colan, in a conclave held at Dame Miniver's that night, "and a health to our squire and our bonny young mistress!"

Loud acclamations and deep draughts gave a welcome to the toast.

"'Tis a strange thing," said the general merchant, "that this matter should have been so long quiet. The times that I've walked by that rift in the cliff yonder, and never seen anything."

"Why?" asked the hostess; "and what would ye expect to see, neighbour Breage? Every winter as passed only packed the sand higher and higher."

"But there might have been a sign, dame, there might have been a sign."

"It shows there was no murder done, at any rate," observed another of the company.

"Still," persisted Breage, "I wonder there was no dream came to point to the place; and especially seeing how hard it has gone with the squire."

"It's like to go hard enough with this Denis or Wyley," Colan remarked. "The fire of Pendar'l was black enough against him, and this story won't tell any way for him."

"But it will for our Edward Owen," said Germoe. "It will turn to his good, and I am glad of it."

"Ay," exclaimed Dame Miniver, "and besides that, I hear talk how he fought for the lady of Pendar'l that night, and beat off some that would harm her."

"We shall have him among us again afore long," said farmer Colan. "And Gabriel will be like to confess all the rights of it before he dies."

"Well," said the pertinacious Breage, "if he confesses to murder, I shall never believe in any sign or token again."

The suspicion here indicated that the smuggler had told only half the truth, prevailed very generally in the hamlet, and many of the villagers thought that he had wilfully thrown the clergyman over the cliff. But we are willing to ascribe the popular feeling to the common love of the worst in criminal matters, and to believe that Wyley was sincere. He was probably prepared for robbery, but not for murder. The revelry at the Trevethlan Arms was protracted till a late hour.

CHAPTER XIV.

Decline all this, and see what now thou art.
For one being sued to, one that humbly sues;
For queen, a very caitiff crowned with care;
For one that scorned at me, now scorned of me;
For one being feared of all, now fearing one;
For one commanding all, obeyed of none.
Thus hath the course of justice wheeled about,
And left thee but a very prey to time;
Having no more but thought of what thou wert,
To torture thee the more, being what thou art.

SHAKSPEARE.

Meanwhile scandal and gossip were still busy with the stolen marriage and its consequences. Mysterious paragraphs had appeared in some of the public prints. If newspapers at that time had been illustrated, there might have been portraits of the bride and bridegroom, or at least of Rhoda, and of the travelling carriage. But the kindred of Asmodeus, who in these days haunt town and country with the implements of Daguerre, and embellish our journals with their woodcuts, had not yet acquired those pictorial aids, and were obliged to content themselves with old-fashioned letterpress. What their descendants may arrive at, especially in alliance with the disciples of Mesmer, to whom distance is no object, and brick and mortar no impediment, it is hard to anticipate. The electric telegraph is likely to be regarded as a slow concern; everybody will know his neighbour's thoughts; the old fable of transparent bosoms will be realized; and the gift of speech will cease to be of any use.

This consummation seems, however, at present rather remote. If we were of a misanthropic turn, and familiar with any good-humoured demon, lame or otherwise, we should trouble him to take us to and fro between the home and haunts of some well-seeming family, and the gloomy chambers where Astræa holds her revels. We should be present one day at the dinner or the ball, and the next day we should go among crumbling papers and musty parchments. We should follow the unconscious prey to the levee or drawing-room, and then we should repair to the dark den, where the spoiler was quietly and assiduously preparing the pit-fall. Often when we look up to the lofty buildings inhabited especially by the servants of Themis, we are led to think of the devices which may there be silently undermining the stability of some well-to-do house, now standing fair and seemly in the eyes of the world.

Far away back, in some ancient record, the lynx-eyed practitioner has lighted upon the trail: step by step he advances, fortifying himself at every pause, until the prize is full in view, and the filing of a bill or the service of a writ informs the unsuspecting victim that his all is at stake; destroying in one moment the whole security of his life, and entangling him in a maze of litigation, to endure possibly for years, and too probably to leave him, even if successful, an impoverished and broken-hearted man. In these days of iron and steam, there is nothing romantic but the law.

And we are not thinking of the mere lovers of chicane, who occasionally disgrace the profession, but of what may happen in the career of the most honourable of its votaries. It was thus that the downfall of Trevethlan was prepared in one office, and that its restoration was now being achieved in another. Little had Randolph dreamed of the plot that was devising against him, and in which the lawyers were but unwitting agents: little did Esther imagine the counter-stroke which was now impending, and to which double weight was to be given by the conduct of her late protégé.

Michael Sinson, baffled in his new attempt against Randolph, had returned sulkily to London. Among the first intelligence which met his eyes in the daily journals was the suicide of his miserable slave. He gnashed his teeth as he read it, and perceived that Rereworth had been in communication with the deceased. Had Everope been a double traitor? Sinson could not free himself from the idea. The ground seemed to be shaking under his feet. After hours of irritating uncertainty, he sought an interview with Mr. Truby, in hope of discovering whether anything had transpired. But he met a very cold reception, and obtained no solution of his anxiety. The lawyer, however, demanded his address, and he, after giving it, went immediately and moved to other quarters.

He mused of coming forward himself as an informant to the other side, but if they were already in possession of the truth, to do so would be merely to place himself in their power. Then he made a futile attempt to gain admission to his former patroness; but being turned from the door with contumely, he thought of his supposed power over her, and fancied that it might yield him both security and profit. With this idea he made his way to Mr. Pendarrel at his office. Here he acquired the knowledge which he had vainly sought from Mr. Truby.

"Do you know, sir," Mr. Pendarrel asked him, "that it is rumoured the evidence at the trial is upset? That they have found relics of the clergyman who really performed that marriage, and that steps are already taken to reverse the judgment?"

Sinson, although he almost expected something of the kind, was staggered by the announcement.

"Now, if this be so," continued Mr. Pendarrel, "it will be strange if you, sir, were not a party to the fraud that will have been perpetrated. Do you mark me?"

He spoke in the cold and deliberate manner which characterized his demeanour whenever he was independent of his wife. Sinson recovered from his first surprise, and assumed an attitude of confidence.

"Whatever I have done," he said, "I have done by the orders of Mrs. Pendarrel. I am now come to receive my recompense."

"You have been well paid, sir," answered Mr. Pendarrel; "there is nothing due to you."

"Perhaps not, for what is past," Sinson said; "but there is for what is to come. You tell me there are rumours of fraud: and I say that Mrs. Pendarrel has authorized whatever has been done. I have her letters. They may be valuable."

"You are a cool scoundrel," said Mr. Pendarrel, "upon my word. But you do not gull me with so simple a device. What hinders me, sirrah, but that I should instantly give you into custody?"

"Nothing, perhaps," was the answer, "but the disagreeable consequences. If you would only be so good as consult my lady, it might change your mind."

"Pooh, sir!" said Esther's husband, "you have overshot your mark. Go now about your business, and don't dare to come here again, or you know the result."

He rang his bell, and ordered the disconcerted intruder to be shown out. Sinson went into the neighbouring park and read over the documents on which he had so fondly relied. And, regarded in the light thrown upon them by Mr. Pendarrel's contempt, they presented him with no consolation in his fall. On the other hand, he had again unwittingly advanced the interests of his detested rival.

Mr. Truby, it may have been observed, frequently in matters of business communicated directly with the wife of his nominal client. When Mr. Pendarrel went from home that day, he found Esther in a state of even unusual depression. She had received a letter from the lawyer, acquainting her there were strong grounds for believing that the main facts on which they had relied at the trial were fabricated for the occasion, and that, as his own character might be implicated by any concealment, he was resolved to probe the matter to the bottom.

"Oh, Gertrude!" said Esther to her constant attendant, "what will become of me? Among them, they are breaking my heart."

She was in this dejected condition when her husband came home. Everything concurred to make him exceedingly desirous to bring about at least a formal reconciliation with the fugitive couple. He read Mr. Truby's letter, and told his wife of the visit he had received that morning.

"And, my dear," said he, "this person would make us accomplices in whatever fraud has been perpetrated."

"Us, Mr. Pendarrel!" Esther ejaculated. "You are jesting, sir, and in a very sorry manner."

But she recollected Michael's threats, and could not help trembling.

"Not I, madam," her husband protested, adopting for a moment her own formal mode of address, "not I, upon my life. Sinson declares that he has letters authorizing all he did, which he pretty plainly admitted to have been more than was honest. And these letters he threatened to use, unless I would purchase them."

"You did not!" Mrs. Pendarrel exclaimed.

"Of course I did not, my dear," was the reply. "I turned his absurd threats upon himself. But it is unpleasant to have these things said. And you see Truby's letter bears out the rumours."

"Ah, me!" Esther sighed, almost wringing her hands, "to what am I fallen?"

"My dear," her husband ventured to urge, "it is time this unhappy matter were settled. After the wrong which will have been done to Mr. Trevethlan"—he started when the name had passed his lips—"after that, I say, we must overlook what has occurred since."

"Do what you will," muttered his wife, "my part in the affair is over. But are you sure they will accept forgiveness? Has he asked for it?"

"Oh yes, dear mother," said Gertrude. "Let me intercede. My poor sister has no peace till she has thrown herself at your feet, and Randolph has none while she is unhappy."

"Well, well," Esther murmured, "I have no more to say. Bring them here, if you will, Gertrude. And since it must be so, the sooner the better."

"And really, my dear Esther," said the husband, "the match is not so disadvantageous after all. You see it will unite the properties, and if Trevethlan is now but a small estate, it is at least unencumbered, which is more than we could say of Tolpeden; and I remember that Mildred was telling me once—"

"Never mind now, papa," said Mrs. Winston, who saw that every word he uttered was a dagger in her mother's heart. "Let me go and prepare my sister to come home."

Indeed, Esther's humiliation required no aggravating circumstances. She was deeply wounded in the tenderest parts of her character. Pride, ambition, and love of rule had all been mortified and abused. And now she succumbed. She resigned any further struggle, and yielded to her victorious foe. Her spirit and mind were alike brought down. After the above conversation she retired to her own room, and drew her miniature from her bosom, and looked long and stedfastly on the tranquil lineaments. Again she reviewed her whole life, and again she fell upon the ever-recurring question—Did he then love me? And she scarcely knew whether an answer in the affirmative would give her most of joy or of regret.

The man who had so long ministered to her will, was in his humbler sphere as completely overthrown. But his feelings were bitter and fierce, and no trace of compunction or repentance was to be found among them. On reconsidering his threats, he clearly saw their futility. When he partly disclosed his story to a scandal-mongering individual with a view to extortion, he was only laughed at for his pains. And he very clearly perceived, that for himself there was nothing in prospect but the penalty of perjury. On every hand he felt that he had been thwarted and defeated. The man whom he knew that he hated had wedded the lady whom Michael fancied he loved, and he foresaw the reconciliation that would make them happy. While he himself, instead of being on the high road to fortune, was an outcast from society, disgraced and infamous.

Yet did one matter detain him in London. One hope remained to save him from absolute despair. By one chance he might even yet retrieve himself, and aspire to a certain position in the world. Wealth, he fancied, would cover a multitude of sins. Cunning had failed him, luck might stand his friend. Day by day he sought the ancient hall, where the wheel of fortune, no longer a mere symbol, dispensed blanks and prizes to a host of care-worn worshippers. And of all that feverish crowd, no votary watched the numbers as they turned up, with more desperate eyes than the peasant of Cornwall. Reckless alike of the jests of the indifferent, of the boisterous glee of the fortunate, and of the execrations of the ruined, he awaited his turn with intense excitement. The great prizes were still in the wheel. He might have realised a very handsome profit on his ticket. But he would scarcely have parted with it for anything short of the highest amount in the list. Little he cared when the revolving cylinder threw out a paltry thousand; no such trifle was an object to him. But he ground his teeth when a number which was not his, appeared in connection with a prize of twenty thousand pounds, and when the very next turn of the wheel declared his ticket—blank—he crushed his hat over his eyes, and slunk out of the hall. He slunk away from town: it was his final leave-taking of the metropolis.

CHAPTER XV.

Oh, days of youth and joy, long clouded,
Why thus for ever haunt my view?
When in the grave your light lay shrouded,
Why did not memory die there too?
Vainly doth hope her strain now sing me,
Whispering of joys that yet remain—
No, never more can this life bring me
One joy that equals youth's sweet pain.

MOORE.

All this time Mildred Trevethlan remained in strict retirement. The only visits which interrupted her solitude were those she occasionally received from Mrs. Winston and from Helen. Gertrude brought intelligence of Mrs. Pendarrel, which was unhappily not of a kind to comfort the repenting fugitive, and her calls were rendered of brief duration by her anxiety to return to the invalid. She could not pretend to assign any other cause than Mildred's flight to their mother's dejection, and her sister trembled to think of the effects of her disobedience. In the many hours when she was necessarily alone, or attended only by Rhoda, she was haunted by fears of the most alarming kind, and whenever Randolph came home after an absence as short as he could make it, he always fancied that his wife's sadness had increased since he left her.

Yet her despondency was lightened for a time when Helen came to see her. For she, gentle and hopeful, dwelt always on the theme to which Gertrude dared not allude. She always promised, or rather predicted, that a reconciliation could not be distant. She bid Mildred to fix her eyes upon that prospect, and to overlook the trouble immediately around her. And upon her brother she urged the duty of obeying the chaplain's injunctions, in their full spirit, and without delay. But Randolph listened to such remonstrances with impatience, and still postponed the day when he would make any advances.

"Let us, at least, be fully restored to our rights," he would say. "Let my father's honour be re-established; let me have a name to bestow upon my bride; and then, when we have exposed the wretched plot by which we were overthrown, we may have the satisfaction of forgiving those who wronged us, and may, if they choose, in turn, accept their forgiveness."

Helen grieved, but could prevail no farther. And, fortunately, the period marked by her brother was fast approaching. Mr. Winter had been already in communication with the friends of Ashton, the clergyman. By good hap, they were able to identify the ring which was found among the buried clothes. This confirmation of the smuggler's story lent it the credit which his character could not give. Everope's confession, attested by Rereworth, had, at least, overthrown the credibility of his previous testimony. And thus the whole case on which the plaintiff in the action had rested his title broke down, and the obscurity which hung around the late Mr. Trevethlan's marriage was finally dissipated.

We need not trouble our readers with the technical proceedings which would terminate in a formal and public reversal of the verdict at Bodmin. Randolph had enjoyed the pleasure of communicating to his wife the approaching result, and, in more kindly temper, was revolving the mode by which they might be reconciled to her friends, when Gertrude came with the message of peace. It was much more than the husband had conceived possible, or than the wife had dared to hope. It left no room for further perverseness. Randolph saw the flush of joy with which Mildred received the offer, and accepted it with eagerness. Mrs. Winston proposed to take them at once to May Fair; and they went without delay.

Without pausing, she conducted them into the presence of Mrs. Pendarrel. And Randolph had taken the mother's offered hand, and Mildred had been pressed to her heart, before either of them well knew what they were about.

Some little awkwardness supervened. Mrs. Winston, with her usual tact, led her sister from the room. Randolph was alone with his father's Esther.

"Mr. Trevethlan," the lady said, after a short silence, and with a faint sigh upon the name, "we have much to forgive each other."

"I have forgiven," Randolph answered. "Let the past be forgotten."

"You have forgiven!" Esther exclaimed mournfully. "Do you know in what you have been wronged?"

"All that is personal to myself has passed from my mind," he replied.

"Ay," said Mrs. Pendarrel, "but there is much that is not personal to yourself. Where is your sister? You are happy in the possession of such a one. Do you know that even to her I have been unkind and unjust?"

"Oh, madam," Randolph said, "do not recall these things. Helen has differed widely from me. Would that I had been guided by her advice!"

"Yet you were right, and she was wrong," observed Esther, who seemed to feel a relief in unburdening her mind. "That letter was intended to try you, and you interpreted it correctly. Helen was more charitable than I deserved."

"Madam," said Randolph, moved by compassion for the humiliation before him, "there had probably been great provocation."

"I do not know," was the meditative answer. "I have tried to persuade myself there was. For if there were not, how shall I ever be justified? Did she tell you, Randolph—did your sister tell you—that I robbed her? See. Do you know this miniature?"

And she showed him the picture of herself. The sight of it reminded her hearer of those dying imprecations which had been so fatal to all his happiness. A dark cloud overspread his brow.

"Ay," said Esther, perceiving the change in his countenance. "You remember, now, that it is not only your peace which I have broken. There is another's for which I have to answer."

"Oh," Randolph exclaimed, "heavy was the task laid upon me, and bitterly indeed have I judged!"

"Listen," Mrs. Pendarrel continued, speaking in tremulous accents. "You know this portrait, but you know not its history. You know not how it once hung from the neck of a wayward and wilful girl. It had often been begged and prayed for, by one who loved her faithfully, fondly—ay, as she believes now—till death. It was taken, or given, in a moment of overpowering tenderness. The vows were plighted, and each had promised to live only for the other. And then she—she, forsooth, idol and votary, worshipped and worshipping—must snap the link, in her petulance and pride, break the heart which adored her, and seek to console her own misery by trampling upon her victim. Oh, Randolph Trevethlan, your father has been deeply avenged. I never forgot that early dream. But I strove to persuade myself that I was forgotten, and excused my own arrogance with the thought. And now this image, which he wore upon his heart—it tells me that he loved me to the last."

"And he died," Randolph said, restraining his emotion, "with words of love upon his lips. 'I mentioned'—it was spoken with his latest breath—'I mentioned Esther Pendarrel. She was once very dear to me'—he then referred to his disappointment—'but I have often thought I was not indifferent to her. If so, she has my pardon.' Oh, madam, I repeat, indeed, something like the words, but it were vain for me to express the feeling with which they were uttered. Alas, I recked not of the promise they contained. I only looked on the dark side of the picture. I chose to make it impossible to ascertain the truth. Entrusted with what was really a message of peace, I have perpetrated animosity. It is I, it is I, who should implore pardon."

Silence followed this speech. Esther fell into a reverie on the past. It was of a more tranquil character than those which of late had caused so much anxiety to her friends. At length it was broken by the return of her daughters. She called Mildred to her side.

"You have deprived me of the power," she said, with a mournful expression strangely at variance with the words, "little rebel, to perform a mother's part. Yet I fain would do it."

She placed Mildred's hand in that of Randolph.

"Take her," she said, "Randolph Trevethlan, and may you know a happiness which has never been mine."

Mildred threw herself into her mother's arms.

"My children," Esther continued, "you will make your home here, till.... And where is Helen?"

Mrs. Winston said, that Helen would perhaps pay her another visit. And in a short time Mrs. Pendarrel quitted the room. She left more of anxiety than of comfort behind her.

"Oh, Gertrude," Mildred exclaimed, "how fearfully she is changed!"

The alteration was indeed too evident to escape notice.

"Do not fear now," Mrs. Winston said; "it has been a trying time, but it is over now. All will be well, Mildred dear."

It was kindly said, and well it would be if the anticipation were fulfilled. But the agitation through which Esther had gone was too likely to leave its traces for many days to come.

In no long time, Randolph set forth on his way to Hampstead, to make his sister and the chaplain partakers of the reconciliation. On his way, he pondered over the train of events in which he had been involved, and admitted the wisdom of Polydore's judgment regarding death-bed injunctions and promises. He could not avoid reverting also to the fatal misunderstanding which, five and thirty years before, had laid the seed of so much bitter fruit. Was the harvest entirely gathered even now? It was a question which rose involuntarily in his mind. And the announcement which he made at Hampstead afforded his hearers a pleasure more unalloyed, it is probable, than any he felt himself. He reminded Mr. Riches of his promise to bestow the nuptial blessing, at the ceremony which would be performed in a few days, and there is no need to say that the chaplain undertook the duty with great delight. And to Helen he delivered an invitation to officiate as bridesmaid, and, in the interval, to occupy her old place at Mrs. Winston's. She accompanied him back to town.

That evening Polydore smoked a pipe with Mr. Peach in a more contented mood than he had enjoyed for some time. He hoped that the sun of Trevethlan was at last emerging from the clouds. The old clerk edified Clotilda, who sat with them rather later than usual, by divers narratives of remarkable elopements, but agreed with the chaplain that marriage in the regular way was a much better thing. And when Miss Peach had retired, the old bachelors fell into their usual humour, and sighed forth the praises of their Rose and Mabel.

"Better, methinks it is," said Polydore in conclusion, "to imagine my beloved Rose smiling upon me from the sky, than to have won her at the expense of another's peace of mind. Better to remember the patience and resignation with which she learnt to watch the stealthy approach of the destroyer, than to reflect upon the rashness which precipitated an unhallowed union. Better to cherish the love which death could not divide, and to look forward to its everlasting reward, than to rush to present enjoyment, and expiate it in future remorse."

The bridegroom invited Rereworth to attend the wedding, as his friend, and Seymour having of course agreed to do so, found an agreeable mode of employing the brief interval by renewing his visits in Cavendish-square. Many a time he went there with the full intention of appearing in his true character as a lover, should an opportunity offer, and as often he departed without having revealed his secret. The question which every man should ask once in his life, rose to his lips continually, and still remained unuttered. For Mrs. Winston saw plainly enough what was the state of affairs, and frequently contrived to leave Rereworth alone with the mistress of his heart. Why did he not avail himself of such an occasion? Was it from timidity, or doubt, or irresolution? No cause had he for fear, no reason for doubt, no wavering to disturb. But in the simple consciousness of being beloved, there was joy so calm and deep, it seemed a pity to ruffle it by any less tranquil emotion. Lie at hot noon under the trees which shade one of the "resting-places" of a great southern river, and you may gaze upon the level water until you cease to wish for the breeze which would cool your brow, because it would also ripple that placid expanse. And Rereworth, although confident of a favourable answer to his petition, yet delayed preferring it, because he was loth to flutter his present peaceful happiness, even by a declaration which would end in enhancing it. So the fond secret was still untold.

That smooth and unvarying affection offered a much fairer prospect of future felicity than the impetuous passion which had united Randolph and Mildred. Even now they felt they were far from serenity. The bridegroom could not overcome the constraint he experienced in the society of his father-in-law; he shrank with instinctive dislike from the Philip Pendarrel whom his own father had denounced in such bitter words; and the feeling was quickened by the cold and calculating prudence of the political manœuvrer. Randolph eagerly cut short all discussions about settlements, and other formalities, and escaped as soon as he could from a companionship which was full of disagreeable associations.

And Mildred was disquieted by the continuing change in her mother, who seemed to lose all care of the present in musing over the past. Yet this was a natural effect of the recent events, and it might reasonably be hoped that no great time would restore Mrs. Pendarrel to tranquillity and resignation.

But during the preparations for the new marriage, we must cast a rapid glance upon the hamlet of Trevethlan.

CHAPTER XVI.

There be bright faces in the busy hall,
Bowls on the board, and banners on the wall;
Far checkering o'er the pictured window, plays
The unwonted faggot's hospitable blaze;
And gay retainers gather round the hearth,
With tongues all gladness, and with eyes all mirth.

BYRON.

The news of the restoration of Randolph to his ancestral towers had already diffused joy through the homes of his tenantry; and the fulfilment of Dame Miniver's prediction respecting his marriage completed the exultation. There was not a heart in the village that was not made lighter by the account of the alliance between Pendarrel and Trevethlan. The castle was busy with the labours of upholsterers and all their tribe, actively employed under the superintendence of the steward and his wife, in renovating some of its ancient splendour; and the Trevethlan Arms rejoiced in their patronage at the close of the day. Old Jeffrey was half frantic with excitement and delight, practising the manœuvre of hoisting and striking a new flag often and often, until it was suggested to him that, by so doing, he deprived the ensign of its significance.

Great preparations were also being made for the reception of the bride and bridegroom. A triumphal arch at the entrance of the green, and another over the gate of the base-court, were ready to be decked with flowers and streamers, when the happy occasion should arrive; for the merry month of May was come, and nature was robing the land in its gayest attire. Mistress Miniver's good-humoured face beamed with delight from sunrise to sunset, and the joyousness of her looks was reflected in the countenances of her neighbours.

Yet this happiness was not unalloyed. There were still not a few absentees from the family hearth, lamenting their turbulence in captivity. Even with respect to them, however, anxiety was mitigated, for it was now understood that Mrs. Pendarrel was inclined to intercede in their behalf. And she had already contributed to the enlargement of Edward Owen. For, inquiring one day, in her languid manner, concerning the mode in which the missing Wyley had been discovered, Randolph mentioned Owen as instrumental in the matter, and she remembered how a man of that name had rescued herself and family from outrage on the night of the fire. And on her representations the young rustic was admitted to bail, with an intimation that his being called up for trial would depend upon his future conduct.

But if he had conceived any hope of finding favour in another quarter, he was disappointed. Mercy Page was as coy as before. Perhaps the very unpopularity of Michael Sinson had contributed to support his cause in the maiden's heart; and certainly the taunts with which she was sometimes assailed were not calculated to change her mind. She had almost sequestered herself from the neighbouring villagers, and either sat at home in her mother's cottage, or walked out late in the evening by herself. On such occasions she was jealously watched, and well it proved for her in the end that it was so.

But Edward was not one of the spies upon her steps. He began to feel chilled by her enduring coldness, and listened more complacently than of old to the words of those who said he might better himself, and particularly to any hints of the kind which fell from the mirthful landlady of the Trevethlan Arms. Farmer Colan once told her, she might not object to change her name; and now a rumour to the same effect became very current in the gossip of the hamlet.

And another topic furnished food to the village scandal-mongers. It was said Michael Sinson had returned to his old country. And it was true. He had left London, writhing under a manifold disappointment, baffled in all his evil desires and devices. Moreover, he suspected that Mr. Truby was strongly inclined to bring him to justice. But unlike his wretched victim, Everope, he was unacquainted with shame, and unstung by remorse. He regretted and resented his want of success; but he rather admired than deplored the subtile villany of his schemes. Sulky and angry, he fled from the metropolis to the dwelling of his grandmother, Wilderness Lodge. Mrs. Pendarrel had not displaced the old gate-keeper. There Michael brooded in silence and retirement for several days, during which his ill-temper was continually fretted, and his evil passions stimulated by the querulousness of the aged fanatic. Shrewd enough was old Maud to see that her favourite had by no means achieved the success which she had foretold for him. He was far away from qualification for that angelic choir, which his mere name appeared to her to entitle him to enter.

The news of his arrival reached the ears of his old flame, probably in some sarcastic shape; and Mercy threw herself in his way. But he thrust her rudely aside, and with so dark a scowl upon his brow that she thought involuntarily of Dame Gudhan's predictions, and shuddered at the recollection. The account of the meeting was soon circulated round the green of Trevethlan, and gave new force to the ill looks which were cast upon the luckless maiden.

But it did not lull the activity, half hopeful and half fearful, with which her steps were dogged.

Meanwhile old Maud harped perpetually on her grandson's failure, and on the attempt to disturb her Margaret's marriage. She was for ever lamenting the injustice done to Michael, and calumniating the house of Trevethlan for its treatment of her favourite daughter. Neither topic was agreeable to Sinson; and at length, irritated at home beyond control, he showed himself among the rural habitations. But he went only to meet with fresh mortification. Every one seemed to know his history. People turned their backs upon the traitor. Children mocked and flouted him. Scorn surrounded him on all sides, and in every shape. Daring to present himself at the Trevethlan Arms, he was ejected with violence and derision, and was hooted and pelted from the village green. And among the foremost of his assailants he recognised his ancient rival. There was nothing for it but to endure the petulance of his fanatical grandmother.

Woe for the "ministering angel!" One hand in Trevethlan had no share in the insults showered that day upon the traitor. One heart in the village refused to believe in the infamy of him it had loved. One voice was heard in sorrow amidst the general execration. One pair of eyes were clouded with tears, where all others flashed with anger. Mercy Page wept for Michael Sinson.

At dusk, the same evening, the village maiden left her mother's cottage, and bent her steps along the quiet lanes to Wilderness Lodge. Now, she thought, was the time to show her devotion, and, if Michael really had gone astray, to call him back to the right path. Now, when all men spoke ill of him, was the time for her to sustain him against their evil report. Hearing of him as prosperous and rising, she had been, comparatively, indifferent. Seeing him abased and insulted, all her early tenderness revived.

She rattled the latch of the gate, and Sinson came out of the lodge. He was astonished at perceiving the visitor, who looked at him with her face half bent down. He returned her glance with a sullen stare, and rudely bade her "begone."

"Michael," she said, "will you not hear me, Michael? Not hear Mercy?"

The soft voice turned the current of the young man's thoughts.

"Know you not what they say of me?" he asked. "Saw you not how I was hunted from among them?"

"I know it all, Michael; but I believe it not. I saw it, and it made me weep."

"Speak not to her," shrieked old Maud, who had come forth to see what her grandson was doing; "speak not to the accursed thing from Trevethlan. Better fortune is in store for my boy. Bid the Armageddon depart."

"And will you walk with me, Mercy, as of old?" the young man asked, without heeding Maud's interruption.

The maiden answered by placing her hand in Michael's arm, and so, side by side, they quitted Wilderness Gate.

Old Maud tottered after them into the road, and gazed in the direction they had taken. She shook the thin locks that hung about her temples, and wrung her hands, and looked up into the sky. The first stars were beginning to twinkle in the gray transparency of twilight.

"Woe's me!" muttered the old crone. "Woe's me! She is leading him to his doom."

And her wild look quite scared a little girl who waited on her, when she returned into the lodge.

We do not care to follow minutely the young couple's evening walk. There is little pleasure in watching the companionship of villany and innocence, even where the latter is triumphant. Fortunately for Mercy, she was well observed that evening. There was a narrow and secluded dell about a mile from Wilderness Lodge, made obscure in the day-time by over-shadowing trees; doubly gloomy, therefore, in the twilight. The brook from Pendarrel Park murmured along it, and a footpath, devious and unfrequented, followed the wanderings of the streamlet. To that sequestered spot, which might seem almost designed for the rambles of lovers, did Sinson guide the steps of her who trusted him with such unsuspecting fidelity. There in her own simple and homely manner she sought to persuade him to be at peace with the world, and to make atonement for any wrong he might have done. But she spoke to an angry and unrepenting nature, and the only answer to her remonstrances made her acquainted with the worthlessness of him in whom she had confided so long.

It was a rude and bitter lesson. "Better he were dead!" has been the exclamation of many a heart deceived like hers. Mercy could no longer hope that the imputations of the villagers were the offspring of rustic jealousy. She hardly knew what happened in the first pain of her discovery. She turned to leave him, for she could do no more. He had followed her, but the watchers interposed. They closed upon the spot in an instant. The maiden was rescued, and the betrayer fled. He glared savagely for one moment upon those who came to save, counted their number, and took to precipitate flight. And the rustics, who had followed the ill-matched maiden with, at least, as much spite as pity, now showed more of the better feeling, and brought her safe, though trembling, home to her mother's cottage.

A warm pursuit was then commenced in the track of her assailant. Summary justice the country-folk thought they would inflict upon the culprit, although he might escape the more regular doom of the law. Many an old ground of exasperation gave vigour to the chase. Many a motive of fear lent wings to its object. He fled over the moors, from carn to carn, and from cave to cave. They drove him at last to the precipices of the Lizard. He retained his strength and activity, and turned them to good account in baffling his pursuers among those beetling cliffs. But, after numerous disappointments, they at length hunted him to bay. They hemmed him in on a ledge from which the rock descended sheer into the sea. Certain that he could not escape, they were, perhaps, negligent in observing his movements. But no one could tell what had become of him, when it was suddenly found that he had disappeared. They looked eagerly into the waves which were dashing against the cliff below; but there they could see no sign. The steepness and height of the rock above utterly precluded the possibility of his having scaled it. Yet there was an unwillingness to believe that he had simply been drowned, and the folks told strange stories of his having been picked up by some boat, and got away to sea. All that was certain was, that he was never heard of again.

The night on which he was lost, his grandmother sat beside the hearth in Wilderness Lodge, swaying herself to and fro in her rocking-chair, and moaning to herself in an under tone. The little girl who attended her was seated opposite on a low stool, and watched her with a feeling of awe, frightened, yet unable to withdraw her eyes from those of her employer, which were fixed and unusually bright.

"Where's my boy?" old Maud might have been heard to mutter. "Where's my own Michael? What is it they tell me of shame? What is it they say he told of my winsome Margaret? Did I hear that the marriage was broken? Na, na, Randolph Trevethlan, thou canst not so sever the ties. Has she not come to claim her own? Let them cross her path that dare. Smiling, did he say? A sweet smiling face? That was my Margaret indeed, but she never smiled at Trevethlan. And would they tell me she went there to shame? Did my Michael speak against her? Na; 't was they that brought her to death; they that will not let her rest in her grave. And why has she woke from her sleep? What comes she back to seek? Why will she not come to me? I was afar when she died. Was it of my own choice? Were we not driven away? Me, and my Michael, and all? Was there one of her kindred left with her? But they are fallen. The dark hour of Trevethlan came. And will they still make us their sport? Where's my own Michael? She came for him the night: the white-faced thing from Trevethlan. What cries did I hear in the sky? What tale did they whisper in my ear?"

Her voice, which had risen occasionally while she spoke, now sank into an inarticulate murmur, and her head dropped, and the rocking of her chair nearly ceased. The little girl looked at her with increasing wonder and dread.

Suddenly Maud raised her head, and after seeming to listen for a moment, cried, "Michael," in one wild and dissonant shriek.

"What voice was that on the wind?" she continued, rising abruptly from the chair. "Who hailed that name?—Michael," she called again, in the same unearthly tone—"didst hear? 'T was his own. Didst hear how it wailed on the wind?—Michael—The waters are sounding in my ears. Didst hear the name, girl?—Drowning.—Ay, it was he—it was he."

Her voice had declined to a hoarse whisper, and her limbs relaxed, and she sank, rather then fell, to the ground. The little girl ran terrified from the lodge to seek for help. When the neighbours whom she summoned returned thither, they found the old woman huddled together in a heap upon the floor. They raised her up, but life had departed: she had rejoined her daughter, Margaret Trevethlan.

CHAPTER XVII.

O blisful ordre, O wedlock precious,
Thou art so mery, and so virtuous,
And so commended, and approved eke,
That every man that holt him worth a leke,
Upon his bare knees oughten all his lif
Thanken his God that him hath sent a wif;
Or elles pray to God him for to send
A wif to last until his lives end.

CHAUCER.

Odious are town-weddings. To our fancy there is something appalling in the splendour with which the ceremony is invested. And it seems to defeat its object; for the festivities which follow the departure of the new-married pair are proverbially dull. But the train of carriages, the cloud of bride-maids, and all the rest of the pomp and parade, appear to us more fitted to gratify the taste of the mob on the pavement, than to show the refinement of the nineteenth century. A solemn rite is converted into a theatrical entertainment. What should be a scene of deep and heart-felt joy becomes a laborious piece of acting. The bridal wreath is sullied by the incense which rises round it. To be sure if there is no heart in the business, if the gist of the union is to be found in the settlements, and the promise to love, honour, and obey is made as a matter of form, then the scenic character of the accessaries is perhaps in keeping, and may serve to throw a decorous veil over the sacrifice. But the village-church is the proper shrine for matrimony. The rustics who make a holiday of the occasion, and come in their Sunday raiment to take respectful leave of their squire's daughter, form a much more seemly retinue, than the gamins and idlers who throng the portico of the London church, staring with rude wonder, and eager for vulgar satire. And is it a childish desire that would fain invest the spot where our fondest hopes were crowned, with a little romance? May we not look forward to future pilgrimages to the altar where we were made the happiest of men? And who could dream of so revisiting St. George's? Nay, even the bells, inaudible in the metropolis, but in the country proclaiming our happiness, will thereby require a new charm in our ears, and their music will awake a new sympathy amidst its many dear and holy associations.

There would, however, as the reader will readily suppose, be little or no display at the re-marriage of Randolph and Mildred. It was fixed to take place at the church belonging to the district in which Mrs. Pendarrel resided. There at the appointed hour, the little party met; and the union, which was before furtive and irregular, received the sanction of Heaven at the hands of Polydore Riches. The ceremony was, perhaps, more impressive than usual, for more serious emotions accompanied its celebration. When it was over, the company returned through a gaping crowd to their carriages, and were driven home to May Fair. And from thence in no great time the bride and bridegroom, after many fond leave-takings, departed to travel by a circuitous route to Trevethlan Castle.

For it had been arranged that Helen, under the chaplain's safe-conduct, should precede them, and be ready to welcome her new sister to the old gray towers. And she carried with her a certain tender reminiscence; for when the time to part approached, Rereworth's love at last over-flowed. A select circle of friends was assembled at Mrs. Pendarrel's to celebrate the event of the day. They were all strangers to Helen, and thus Seymour was able to appropriate her to himself. Even this little party was a novelty to her, and served to prolong the excitement caused by the ceremony of the morning. In the midst of a rapid and animated conversation, some allusion to the happiness of the married couple, which reached Seymour's ear, threw him completely off his guard.

"Happy!" he exclaimed. "Oh, dearest Miss Trevethlan, may not a like happiness be mine? May not I also—"

His voice sunk into a whisper, but his prayer was heard. And the ice being thus broken, Rereworth told hurriedly of all he desired, and he might read in Helen's flushed cheeks and downcast eyes, that he need not fear. He had accepted an invitation from Randolph to spend a portion of the ensuing long vacation at the castle, and then he flattered himself he might appear as Helen's recognised suitor.

In the afternoon Mr. Riches returned to his quarters at Hampstead, to spend his last night at the metropolis. Long was the session, which he held there with the old clerk. A hint had made Cornelius and his sister acquainted with the scene of the marriage, and they had been unobserved, but not unobservant, spectators of the ceremony. And for many a day after Polydore's departure, the two old bachelors maintained a constant correspondence, in which they discussed the merits of old essayists, and criticised the beauties of old plays. Sister Clotilda and her brother never seemed to grow older than they were when Randolph and Helen dwelt beneath their roof. Sometimes their old lodger invited them through the chaplain to make a tour to Trevethlan Castle, promising to shew them all the wonders of the land. But Cornelius, though he did not appear to age, grew more and more fond of the flags of the metropolis, and could not be prevailed upon to attempt so long an excursion. "I am no traveller," he once wrote to Mr. Riches. "Twenty or twenty-five miles of nice quiet road, with green hedges and comfortable inns, a cow or two here and there, and now and then a pig, that is all the country I like. London is my pleasure. I affect a bit of enthusiasm to strangers about this village of Hampstead, but I should like it better without the hill." And so peace and farewell to the peachery.

The arrival of Helen and the chaplain occasioned much rejoicing in the hamlet of Trevethlan, but the main demonstration was of course reserved for the coming of the young squire and his bride. And a proud day it was for old Jeffrey, when their carriage dashed over the green amidst the cheers of the villagers, and he finally hoisted the family flag to the top of its staff.

There was firing and feasting, and dancing, in the hamlet and the castle; the great hall was thrown open to all comers, and the rivalry between Trevethlan and Pendarrel was drowned in flowing bowls, and forgotten in the unions of the mazy measure. And night had long hung her pall over the sea, before silence reigned in the towers on the cliff.

And here, perhaps, we might drop the curtain. But the reader will not be displeased at a rapid glance over some of the years which have elapsed since that happy day. The tranquillity which succeeded to the first exuberance of joyousness, was not unchequered with feelings of a more pensive cast.

The hamlet, indeed, throve under the renewed splendour of the castle. Mrs. Miniver removed the boards from the windows in the wings of the hostelry, and re-opened the rooms which had so long been closed. Nay, she was no longer Mrs. Miniver, having submitted to the change at which farmer Colan had hinted, and taken unto herself a husband. Edward Owen was the fortunate man. True, he was a dozen or fifteen years younger than his buxom bride, but she was more youthful in spirit than in age. The match seemed to turn out as comfortably as either party could desire. It is probable that the lady retained possession of her bunch of keys.

His old sweetheart, Mercy, was not to be tempted into wedlock. Helen renewed her confidence with the fair rustic, and introduced her to Mildred. But she never forgot her unworthy lover. She scarcely believed he was lost to her forever; but sometimes felt a transient fear that, in a foreign land, he might have found the fate predicted for him by the old sibyl of St. Madron's Well. But no intelligence ever arrived, either to confirm or to contradict the maiden's apprehensions.

Mildred had been only a very short time at the castle when she was introduced to Merlin's Cave. We cannot close our labours without reverting for a moment to the grotto, which possessed so many associations for Randolph and Helen. Few of our readers, we would believe, will not, at some period of their lives, have had a Merlin's Cave of their own. Seated under the little canopy of rock, the young bride learned the traditional ballad of her new home, and trusted that it might never again be applicable to the fortunes of the family. There too she became acquainted with the black-letter lore, which of old was the delight of her husband and sister; and there in long detail she heard the story of their early ambition. On Mid-summer eve they all repaired thither to witness the lighting of St. John's fires. Then as the shades of evening fell over the sea, long streams of radiance rose into the sky from all the numerous villages surrounding the beautiful bay. From Carn Dew over Lamorna Cove all round to Cudden Point, the landscape sparkled with the festive bonfires. The spectators might hear the sounds of distant revelry borne from afar over the waters, and echoed more loudly from the green of their own hamlet.

At the trial of the prisoners charged with the incendiarism at Pendarrel, it was suggested, in their defence, that the fire was occasioned by the lightning. Gabriel Denis kept his own counsel. And the doubt so raised, combined with certain powerful intercession, availed to mitigate the extreme penalties of the law. Of the criminals, some were transported for various terms, and others imprisoned. Gabriel's little girl was brought up at Trevethlan Castle, and caused no small trouble, with her hot Spanish blood. But it was endured, in remembrance of the confession of the witness, Wyley.

The long vacation brought Rereworth to the castle, and few days had passed when he communicated to Randolph, Helen's sanction of his dearest aspirations. And the brother rejoiced at the news, and warmly congratulated both himself and his friend. Seymour thought himself fortunate in obtaining a house, with pleasant grounds attached, in the neighbourhood where he had first met the lady of his love; and thither, in the space of a few months, he had the joy of conducting her as his bride. And Helen cordially accepted her new abode, shared her husband's hopes, and encouraged his professional ambition. She might be unable to repress an occasional regret for the land of her infancy, childhood, and youth, but the feeling was never visible in the company of her friend, lover, and husband

Some years elapsed before Mrs. Pendarrel revisited the country of her ancestors. She was content to see Mildred and Randolph, when they came to stay a while with the Winstons or Rereworths, which they did every spring. She had subsided into a moping kind of melancholy, which annoyed her husband and grieved her children. The only circumstance which ever seemed to dissipate it was the growing good understanding between Gertrude and Mr. Winston. This appeared to remove some of the weight which oppressed her mind. And it showed, that if those who are cast together by accident, or even against their will, will study one another's merits, instead of seeking for faults and dwelling on discomforts, happiness may be found in circumstances where least it might be expected beforehand. It was a lesson which Gertrude learned with a thankful heart.

The visits of the spring were returned in the autumnal holidays, when a joyous throng of young people met regularly, in the course of time, at Trevethlan Castle. Holidays they were indeed. The Rereworths were always there, and most often the Winstons. Then the base court resounded with the glee of children, with a confusion of tongues and of names worthy of Babel. Griffith, declining gently into the vale of years, presided over the gambols. Sometimes the ancient sport of archery, the loss of which is so much deplored by Cornwall's old surveyor, Carew, was revived, and all the neighbouring country met to try their skill at the butts; while the little ones, escaping from the mild dominion of Polydore Riches, who was now, in green old age, the teacher of a new generation, mimicked the proceedings of their seniors, with bows and arrows suited to their years.

Pendarrel Hall remained a ruin. The estate was settled upon Mildred and her husband, and it seemed unnecessary to maintain two large residences upon the united property. The flower-garden surrounding it was allowed to run to waste, and the blackened walls continued standing, mournful memorials of an outrage which had exiled several of its perpetrators from their native land. Ivy was planted around the foundations, and at some future day, the ruin might become a picturesque feature in the landscape.

It was the doom which its mistress, in the opening of this narrative, anticipated for the towers of Trevethlan. The menace or the desire had been deeply avenged. But Esther was not the only person upon whom the storm left traces of its passage. Mildred was often visited with feelings of compunction and remorse, and the cloud which they brought upon her brow called down a similar shadow upon Randolph's. And when her mother survived Mr. Pendarrel, and in her loneliness accepted the shelter of Trevethlan Castle, her aspect and demeanour were a constant source of self-reproach to her daughter. Without being actually imbecile, she required minute attention. She was very rigid and exacting in all the little business of life. Her temper was uncertain, and it was difficult to gratify her fleeting wishes. At times it might be thought that she remembered how she should have been mistress of the castle, and imagined for a brief space that she in fact occupied that position.

Frequently, too, she fell into long and silent reveries, and then it was that the melancholy which overspread her countenance, caused the greatest anxiety to her children. She always wore the miniature of herself, and used to gaze at it, with a vacant but mournful expression, for an hour at a time. But at length they found a means of diverting her attention. She attached herself particularly to her eldest grand-daughter; and whenever she sank into too prolonged a train of musing, the little girl crept softly to her knees, and took her hand. And then Esther awoke from her dream of the past, and smoothed the dark hair upon the child's forehead, and told many little stories, which delighted the young listener.

Rarely did it happen that this manner of relief failed of effect. But sometimes Esther's abstraction was too deep to yield. At such seasons she murmured to herself in low tones. And the little girl caused her mother a bitter pang, by unwittingly telling her that, on one of these occasions, grandmamma was only repeating, over and over again, and without intermission—

"PENDAR'L AND TREVETHLAN SHALL OWN ONE NAME."

THE END.

Milton Keynes UK
Ingram Content Group UK Ltd.
UKHW040311181024
449757UK00005B/489